O9-AID-705

ALL ABOUT
SALADS & DRESSINGS

Joy
of Cooking

ALL ABOUT
SALADS & DRESSINGS

IRMA S. ROMBAUER
MARION ROMBAUER BECKER
ETHAN BECKER

PHOTOGRAPHY BY TUCKER & HOSSLER

SCRIBNER
NEW YORK • LONDON • TORONTO • SYDNEY • SINGAPORE

SCRIBNER
1230 Avenue of the Americas
New York, NY 10020

WELDON OWEN INC.
Chief Executive Officer: John Owen
President: Terry Newell
Chief Operating Officer: Larry Partington
Vice President, International Sales: Stuart Laurence
Publisher: Roger Shaw
Creative Director: Gaye Allen
Associate Publisher: Val Cipollone
Associate Editor: Anna Mantzaris
Consulting Editors: Barbara Ottenhoff,
Judith Dunham, Norman Kolpas
Designers: Sarah Gifford, Lisa Schulz
Photo Editor: Lisa Lee
Production Director: Stephanie Sherman
Production Manager: Chris Hemesath
Production Assistant: Donita Boles
Studio Manager: Brynn Breuner
Food Stylist: Dan Becker
Step-by-Step Photographer: Mike Falconer
Step-by-Step Food Stylist: Andrea Lucich

Joy of Cooking All About series was designed
and produced by Weldon Owen Inc.,
814 Montgomery Street, San Francisco,
California 94133

Set in Joanna MT and Gill Sans

Separations by Bright Arts Singapore
Printed in Singapore by Tien Wah Press (Pte.) Ltd.

10 9 8 7 6 5 4 3 2 1

Library of Congress Cataloging-in-Publication Data
is available.

ISBN 0-7432-1501-X

Recipe shown on half-title page: *Tart Green Salad, 18*
Recipe shown on title page: *Tunisian-Style Carrot Salad, 35*

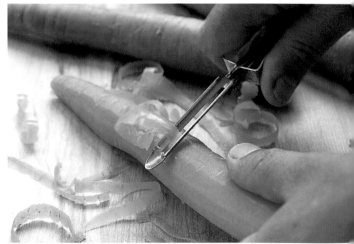

CONTENTS

FOREWORD

"There is an ever-increasing demand for salads of all kinds, and a greater and greater appreciation of their contribution to our gastronomical enjoyment and our improved health." Those words, written several decades ago by my mom and Granny Rom in an early edition of the Joy of Cooking, *seem prophetic today, as salads of all kinds form such a vital part of our cooking and our eating.*

Recognizing the ongoing popularity of salads, this volume of the All About *series offers recipes for salads in all their vast variety, from simple mixtures of greens or fruits to composed and molded salads to main-course creations featuring meat, poultry, or seafood. Informative text throughout the book tells you everything you need to know about such topics as choosing greens and making dressings.*

You might notice that this collection of kitchen-tested recipes is adapted from the latest edition of the Joy of Cooking. *Just as our family has done for generations, we have worked to make this version of* Joy *a little bit better than the last. As a result, you'll find that some notes, recipes, and techniques have been changed to improve their clarity and usefulness. Since 1931, the* Joy of Cooking *has constantly evolved. And now, the* All About *series has taken* Joy *to a whole new stage, as you will see from the beautiful color photographs of finished dishes and clearly illustrated instructions for preparing and serving them. Granny Rom and Mom would have been delighted.*

I'm sure you'll find All About Salads & Dressings *to be both a useful and an enduring companion in your kitchen.*

Enjoy!

   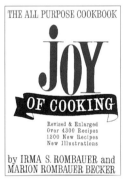

Ethan Becker pictured with his grandmother, Irma von Starkloff Rombauer (left), and his mother, Marion Rombauer Becker (right). Irma Rombauer published the first Joy of Cooking *at her own expense in 1931. Marion Rombauer Becker became coauthor in 1951. Joy as it has progressed through the decades (from top left to bottom right): the 1931 edition with Marion's depiction of St. Martha of Bethany, said to be the patron saint of cooking, "slaying the dragon of kitchen drudgery"; the 1943 edition; the 1951 edition; the 1962 edition; the 1975 edition; and the 1997 edition.*

About Salads

Although the term *salad* once meant nothing more than greens and herbs seasoned with salt, today's salads are made from almost every sort of vegetable, meat, poultry, fish, pasta, grain, or legume, raw or cooked, cold or warm, tied together by a flavorful dressing. Every step in creating a salad, from selecting ingredients to serving it, allows for the cook's imagination.

A plate of marinated vegetables will spark the appetite before the main course. Salads can also replace vegetable side dishes. Tangy cole slaw and creamy potato salad make perfect partners to barbecued foods. And finally, a simple green salad is an excellent way to refresh the palate after the main course of a large dinner and a perfect preparation for the dessert to come. Innovative combinations of salad greens paired with grilled or roasted meat, fish, or shellfish are gaining ground as full-fledged entrées in our quest for healthful and lighter ways of eating.

All this freedom can be seen as a tribute to American creativity as well as to the variety of foods available to us.

However, it is at its best practiced with some restraint. Care should be taken not to pack too many diverse ingredients into one salad. Each element should be chosen for its unique contribution of flavor, texture, and appearance. Too many tastes combined without thought results in a clamor of flavors and textures that no one will enjoy.

Tossed Salads

The relatively simple effort required to produce an outstanding salad is nowhere more evident than in the mother of all salads—the tossed salad. Tossed salads are often referred to as green salads, garden salads, or mixed salads, and while there may be other additions—croutons, herbs, cheese—the greens are paramount. All too often we are served limp greens topped with a dollop or two of bottled dressing, a few croutons, and a wedge of tomato, all crowded onto an undersized plate. Anyone who has ever enjoyed a garden-fresh mix of cool, crisp greens dressed with a light coat of a well-balanced vinaigrette understands the distinction. A well-made tossed salad is never an afterthought but rather a carefully orchestrated part of the entire meal.

In its simplest form, a green salad is composed of one kind of fresh lettuce dressed with the best-quality oil and vinegar you can manage. In a more complex presentation, it is a mix of carefully selected greens garnished with seasonings, vegetables, meat, or fish and tossed with a specially tailored dressing. Whatever the case, keep in mind that the type of tossed salad you prepare should depend on what role it plays in your menu.

Greens

ARUGULA

Also called Italian cress and found across the United States, arugula is a member of the mustard family. (The Italians call it *rucola*, the French *roquette*, and the English rocket.) It has a tender leaf, a pungent peppery bite, and the scent of pine. Some varieties have smooth-edged leaves, and others have serrated leaves. The spiciness of arugula intensifies as it ages and also varies considerably from bunch to bunch. Dark green in color, arugula is delicious alone or as an accent in mixed green salads. It also combines well with legumes, especially white beans, and other vegetables. Tiny arugula blossoms are gorgeous, white or yellow with brown markings, and are not to be missed. They make a handsome, pungent addition to salads.

BABY GREENS

While many leafy green vegetables are served in cooked form when they attain maturity, they are also sold in their infant stage, when they are delicate in texture and flavor. They can then be eaten raw in salads. Try some of the following.
Amaranth: Young green-leaf amaranth is tender, with an intense spinachy taste (another name for it is Chinese spinach). The red varieties have the same flavor and brighten a salad nicely. **Beet Greens:** Only the tiniest of these can be eaten raw, for they soon become too tough to be palatable. If you have a garden, trim them when you thin the beets and add them to salads. They provide a fresh taste and a faint echo of the flavor of beets. **Bok Choy:** Also called pak choi, this is a member of the mustard cabbage family; it comes in loose heads of fleshy stalks and broad leaves, with stalks that are white or green, thin or broad. Leaves may be light to dark green, thick or thin, cupped or flat. Baby bok choy is a miniature, delicately flavored bunch of leaves with small stalks, about 4 inches long. **Collards:** These flat, blue-green, cabbage-flavored leaves are sweetest when grown in cold climates and picked after a frost. **Kale:** Most culinary kales have ragged or frilled blue, magenta, or grayish leaves. Kales have a delicate cabbage taste and, like collards, are sweetest after a frost. Kale makes a beautiful garnish when mature and can be used as a green when very young. **Komatsuna:** Also known as mustard spinach, this Japanese green has thick dark green leaves. Its flavor combines the blandness of cabbage and the bite of mustard. The young stalks are also delicious. **Mustard Greens:** This term is a catchall for any leafy green in the mustard family not otherwise identified by name. They may be broad and smooth or fringed and curled, dark green or light green or purple, hot and pungent or mild and sweet.

Clockwise from center: baby bok choy, collard greens, mustard greens, arugula, kale

Mustards can be eaten raw only when very small. They add a strong peppery flavor to a salad. **Swiss Chard:** This green has long, flat, celery-like stalks with large, coarse leaves at the top. Red Swiss chard, also known as rhubarb chard, has ruby-colored stalks. The stems have a delicate, celery-like taste, and the leaves have a hearty, spinachlike flavor. Chard has an affinity with citrus, so use a lemon dressing or add segments of orange or grapefruit to the salad. **Turnip Greens and Broccoli Rabe (Rapini, Broccoli Rape, Broccoli Raab, Broccoli di Rape):** These are forms of turnip leaves (*rapa* means turnip in Italian) and, when young, can be used like arugula. They have a mustardy bite, sometimes with a touch of sweetness.

BELGIAN ENDIVE

This green is the blanched head of a variety of chicory known as *witloof* (Dutch for "white leaf"), which is grown in darkness to preserve its very light color and mild flavor. The heads resemble young unshucked corncobs, creamy white with pale yellow tips. The leaves are both tender and crisp and have a distinctly clean, mildly bitter flavor. Belgian endive blends well with tart greens, such as radicchio and arugula and contrasts equally well with soft, delicate lettuces, such as Boston or Bibb.

CABBAGE

Because green cabbages tend to be bitter in spring and summer, care should be exercised in mixing them with other tart greens. Winter cabbages, especially Savoy cabbage, are sweeter. Finely shredded red cabbage is a salad basic, used for color and texture for years before radicchio and other exotic greens appeared in our markets. Varieties of Chinese cabbage suitable for salads are michihili, whose crisp, mild, dark green leaves grow in a cylinder like a tall, slender head of romaine lettuce, and Napa or Nappa, whose pale ruffled leaves and crunchy ribs have a mild, slightly nutty flavor.

CELERY LEAVES

Chopped celery stalks appear in many kinds of salads, but the leaves are also good-tasting and leave a hint of pepper. The pale whitish green ones at the heart are best.

CELTUCE

Also known as stem or asparagus lettuce, this is an Asian lettuce grown for its thick, succulent stalk. It tastes a bit like water chestnuts. Very young leaves can be used in salads.

CHICORY

A group of bitter greens in the sunflower family. See Belgian Endive, Curly Endive, Escarole, and Radicchio.

CRESSES

Common cresses, which belong to the mustard family, have leaves ranging from faintly peppery to searing hot in character. Watercress, the mildest and most familiar form, has crisp stems and glossy, dime-sized, dark green leaves. The stems as well as the leaves are edible. Garden cress is softer in texture but similar to watercress in taste. Curly cress leaves are lacy, like those of flat-leaf parsley, but extremely pungent. Upland cress is similar to watercress, but if grown in hot weather, it becomes so strong as to be nearly inedible.

CURLY ENDIVE

A variety of chicory, this has coarse, prickly, dark green leaves with a pleasant tang. The terms *curly endive* and *frisée* are used interchangeably, though most often what is labeled "frisée" has small, tender, lacy, pale green leaves with white centers and has a mild tartness and a more delicate taste than other chicories.

DANDELION GREENS

A very tart green with jagged-edged leaves that look like arrows. Young, tender leaves less than 6 inches long are the least tart and are ideal in salads. Both raw and cooked, dandelion greens have a rich, bracing flavor and are worth buying when they appear in the market.

ESCAROLE

Eaten both raw and cooked, this member of the chicory family has broad, irregularly shaped flat leaves with slightly curled edges, like the leaves of butterhead lettuce. The leaves are dark green at the top and grow paler as they approach the stem. The leaves have a pronounced tartness and a firm, chewy texture.

GOOD KING HENRY

Also called allgood or wild spinach, these spade-shaped leaves, often the first greens of spring, have a faint spinachlike flavor but are not related to spinach. Good King Henry mixes nicely with tender red-leaf lettuces.

HERBS AND FLOWERS

Add leaves or blossoms whole, tear them into bite-sized pieces, or cut them into ribbons. To add in quantity as a salad green: angelica, any basil, chervil, cilantro, dill, Florence fennel leaves, lemon balm, lovage, marjoram, any mint, any parsley, any sage, salad burnet, sweet cicely, tarragon. To use sparingly as an accent: ambrosia, anise, anise hyssop, caraway, epazote, garlic, garlic chives, Greek oregano, hyssop, Mexican oregano, mitsuba, perilla or shiso, rosemary, any savory, any thyme, Vietnamese coriander. These flowers add flavor: clove pinks, elderberry, lavender (sparingly), lemon, mustard, nasturtium, rose, rosemary, scented geranium, society garlic, sweet woodruff, violets.

LETTUCES

There are hundreds of individual varieties of lettuce—all from one of four general categories, classified by the shape and growth habit of the lettuce. **Butterhead:** Tender and delicately flavored, with soft ruffled leaves gathered together into small, round, rather loose heads. Familiar varieties include Bibb, Boston, butter, limestone, and red tip. Bibb is more delicate-tasting than the larger Boston. The subtly sweet, buttery flavor of these lettuces combines well with stronger-flavored greens and is also lovely on its own. **Iceberg:** Also known as crisphead, iceberg lettuce has a compact, smooth round head that varies from pale green in the center to medium green on the outside and is dependably crisp, crunchy, very heavy in the hand, tightly packed, and compact. This lettuce has a distinct and attractive flavor, ships well, and can be torn, shredded, or sliced like cabbage. It is also available year-round. **Looseleaf:** Tender, mild, mellow, and soft, these lettuces are also known as "bunching" or "cutting" lettuces. They have sprawling, crisp yet tender leaves with sweet and refined flavors and are at their best in the spring. The leaves grow loosely bunched and may have ruffled edges and/or red tips. The many varieties of looseleaf lettuces include green leaf, red leaf, and oakleaf. These lettuces are wonderful to eat on their own and also blend well with stronger-tasting greens. **Romaine or Cos:** This is a cylindrical, upright lettuce with stiff, elongated leaves, crisp center ribs, a rather juicy but relatively coarse texture, and a pleasantly

Clockwise from top center: chard, Savoy cabbage, Belgian endive, red butter lettuce, butter lettuce, broccoli rabe, radicchio, frisée

Clockwise from top left: bok choy, orache, mâche, pea shoots, tatsoi

assertive taste. The outer leaves are usually darker in color than the inner leaves and have a stronger flavor. It is also available in red.

MÂCHE

A member of the chicory family, this exceptional green is also called rapunzel, feldsalat, lamb's lettuce, and corn salad because it often grows in cornfields. Very delicate, sweet, and nutty, it is also very expensive because it is highly perishable. The clusters are small, made up of smooth, velvety, tongue-shaped green leaves. It is marvelous served alone or in combination with other delicate greens and herbs.

MESCLUN

This is not a type of green, but the name given to a mixture of salad greens that has recently become very popular. The term comes from the Provençal word for "mixture," and the idea comes from the practice common throughout Europe of gathering a variety of young field greens and mixing them in a salad. In the United States, mesclun has become a catchall term, meaning any assortment of edible greens that are delicate and mild enough to be eaten raw. The idea is to create a balance between strong-flavored greens like arugula or mizuna, and subtle greens like baby lettuces.

MINER'S LETTUCE

Also called claytonia, these are small, slightly cupped, triangular-shaped leaves with tiny flowers in their centers. Their flavor is fresh, rather like mild spinach.

MIZUNA

Of Asian origin, and one of the most delicately flavored of the mustards, mizuna has dark green, feathery leaves that are delightful tossed with flowers and a light dressing flavored with sesame oil. Baby mizuna is an essential ingredient in mesclun.

ORACHE

These arrow-shaped leaves, sometimes called mountain spinach, have a mild spinach flavor.

PEA SHOOTS

The first 3 to 5 inches of a snow pea vine, including the vine itself, tendrils, leaves, pods, and sometimes flowers, are considered the pea shoot. They are popular in the cooking of Shanghai and Vietnam and now appear in our markets. Freshly picked, these are crisp, with a light pea flavor. They are exquisite in salads and, though delicate, hold their own with stronger flavors.

PURSLANE

Although considered a weed in most of the United States, this green has been eaten for centuries throughout India, Turkey, and parts of the Middle East. It resembles a small creeping jade plant. Leaves of the Goldgelber variety are large and golden. Purslane has juicy stalks and small oval leaves with a tart lemony flavor.

RADICCHIO

There are two varieties of this Italian chicory, one with a round head that resembles a small tender cabbage, the other with elongated leaves. Both are a beautiful magenta-mauve color with ivory streaks, and both have a pleasantly bitter, slightly peppery flavor. Radicchio combines well with both mild and assertive greens and adds stunning color to any salad.

SHUNGIKU

Also known as chrysanthemum leaves or garland chrysanthemum, these are the uniquely tasty, almost perfumed leaves of a type of chrysanthemum.

SORREL

Garden sorrel comes up early in spring and lasts until snow crushes its stalks; where winters are mild, sorrel is green all year long. The leaves and stalks look like bright green spinach, but that is where the resemblance ends. Sorrel's flavor is its own—intensely lemony and exhilarating on the tongue. It is wonderful in salads, but use it discreetly because its flavor can overwhelm. Sorrel is in season spring, summer, and fall, but its leaves are most tender in spring.

SPINACH

With its clean, astringent freshness, the flavor of spinach is the reference point for many green leaves. Whether crinkled or flat (the latter are more delicate in flavor), spinach leaves are a versatile, valuable salad green. Include the stems, chopping them neatly, and if the pink roots are still attached, drop them in too for their crunch. Spinach is available all year at the market, but its peak season is the cool of spring and fall.

TATSOI

A ground-hugging member of the mustard family, this is also known as rosette bok choy because its leaves grow like rose petals. The rounded leaves are thick and very dark green and have an assertive mustard flavor esteemed by the Chinese.

GREENS SUBSTITUTION CHART

If you cannot locate a particular green called for in the salad recipes, you can almost always find a substitute.

Mild Greens
Butterhead Lettuces
Crisphead Lettuces
Looseleaf Lettuces
Romaine Lettuces
Celery Leaves
Celtuce
Mâche, or Corn Salad

Slightly Tart Greens
Arugula
Belgian Endive
Collards
Curly Endive
Dandelion Greens
Escarole
Kale
Mizuna
Watercress
Young Romaine Lettuce Hearts

Tart Greens
Arugula
Broccoli Rabe
Curly Cress
Curly Endive
Escarole
Mustard Greens
Radicchio
Radish Leaves
Turnip Greens
Upland Cress

Mild Cabbages
Bok Choy
Collards
Kale
Komatsuna

Spinach
Amaranth
Beet Greens
Chard
Good King Henry
Komatsuna
Miner's Lettuce

Crisp Greens
Cabbages
Iceberg Lettuce
Pea Shoots
Purslane

RULES FOR PREPARING GREENS FOR A SALAD

• To begin with, buy the freshest greens with crisp leaves, free of brown spots on leaves or stems. When available, greens still attached to their roots are usually more intense in flavor than those severed at the stem.

• Use greens as soon as possible after buying them. If you have to store them, remove any leaves that are wilted or show signs of decay and take off any rubber or metal bands holding greens together. Unwashed greens will keep for 3 to 4 days at most. (If the greens wilt slightly, they can often be revived by soaking them in ice-cold water for 3 to 5 minutes, drying them well, then placing them in the refrigerator for 30 minutes or so.) Store greens in the vegetable bin of your refrigerator in a plastic bag with holes poked in it.

• Properly washing, drying, and chilling salad greens is the indispensable first step in any salad. No marvel of ingredients or perfection of dressing can mask or make up for sand or dirt on salad greens. Likewise, inadequately dried greens, left full of water, will render the entire salad soggy and flavorless, since dressing can cling only to dry leaves. Unchilled greens rapidly become limp and lose their flavor.

• Always handle greens carefully, so as not to bruise them. The easiest way to wash them is to separate the leaves and place them in a large bowl or sink full of cold water, swish them around for 30 seconds or so (**1**), then lift them from the water gently so that the dirt and grit remain in the water. Repeat the process until the water is clear; one dunking may do for relatively clean greens such as red-leaf lettuce, while spinach, which is notoriously sandy, may take three or four. If you are in doubt, the surest way to remove sand and grit is to expose the entire surface of each leaf to cold running water for a brief time. This takes a bit longer but yields the reward of an entirely sand-free salad.

• For drying, salad spinners are a wonderful convenience. Overcrowding a salad spinner, however, will both bruise the greens and hinder the device's ability to dry them adequately. A spinner about one-half to two-thirds full will work perfectly every time (**2**). Alternatively, dry greens by tossing lightly in a colander. In either case, it will probably be necessary to wrap them in paper towels for the final drying. Whatever the method, once dried, the greens should be well chilled to render them crisp.

• Once they are washed and dried, store greens in whole form, tearing or cutting them only when you are about to make the salad. They should be placed in the coolest part of the refrigerator, which is usually one of the vegetable storage bins, where they will keep well for 2 but not more than 3 days. If you are serving the salad the same day, the ideal container for washed and dried greens is your salad bowl. Line it with paper towels, add the greens (**3**), cover with two layers of moistened paper towels, and seal the bowl tightly with plastic wrap or aluminum foil. Otherwise, put them into a plastic bag with holes poked in it.

• To assemble the salad, sort through the greens, discarding any tough stems or wilted spots, and gently tear them by hand into small uniform pieces. Especially crisp greens can be sliced or shredded with a knife.

Dressing Salads

The time to dress green salads is always at the very last minute. Once dressed, greens lose their charm by becoming limp if they sit too long.

To dress a salad, place the greens in a bowl large enough to hold them spaciously. Whether combined beforehand or actually mixed in the bowl, pour the dressing or its ingredients down the side of the bowl so that it forms a puddle at the bottom. The tossing can now be done with clean hands, a pair of tongs, a couple of ordinary wooden kitchen spoons, or the oversized fork and spoon known as a salad set.

Whatever implements you choose, the tossing action is always the same. In all cases, reach into the bottom of the bowl and gently lift the greens upward so that the topmost greens fall to the bottom. Gently repeat this action until all the leaves have had their turn moving across the bottom of the bowl and all the dressing is distributed. If salt, pepper, or any other dry condiments are to be added, sprinkle them lightly over the greens as you toss. Each leaf should glisten with just enough dressing to enhance its flavor. Too much dressing will destroy the bright freshness that is a hallmark of a good salad. It is always best to start with too little dressing and add more if necessary.

Specialty dressings are included with some of the salad recipes in this book, but see *About Salad Dressings, 105,* for others. As a general rule, thick, creamy dressings work better with sturdy greens, and simple dressings often match up best with complex salads with many ingredients. Allow 1½ to 2 cups loosely packed washed and dried greens and 2 to 3 tablespoons dressing per person (less for vinaigrettes and more for creamy dressings). Since we often prepare salads for more than one, figure ½ cup vinaigrette (or ¾ cup creamy style) for 4 servings.

Serving Tossed Salads

Simple salads belong after the main course or as a side dish, while more complex salads come first as an appetizer or stand on their own as a main course. Some type of bread, breadstick, or cracker complements most salads. In all except the most informal settings, serve separate salad plates or bowls to keep the dressing from running into other flavors in the meal and vice versa. Chilling the plates or bowls helps maintain the desired crisp, cool character of the greens. Generally, serve all salads on large plates or in bowls so that one's salad does not tumble onto the table or one's lap. Cutting or tearing all salad ingredients into pieces no larger than bite-sized will make for gracious dining as well.

Caring for Salad Bowls

Well-seasoned wooden salad bowls are sometimes ascribed a sacred inviolability by salad fanciers. Soap and a sponge supposedly must never touch them. We think this idea is mistaken. The residue left after wiping the bowl with only a damp cloth tends to become rancid and can mar the flavor of subsequent salads, especially if assertive oils, such as walnut and hazelnut oils, are used. We recommend a bowl made of glass or pottery with a glazed surface. A wooden bowl that is sealed with a food-grade varnish will also work well. All should be scrupulously cleaned after each use. Whether the bowl is glass, ceramic, or wood, it should be large and wide enough to toss at least a quart of salad greens with ease.

PACKING SALADS FOR A PICNIC

For a picnic or a camping trip, wash and dry the greens (iceberg lettuce will stay crispest the longest), then chill them in a large plastic bag. Take the dressing along in a separate container.

ABOUT **GREEN** SALADS

A plate of fresh greens captures the very essence of the salad-making art. The elements are simple: crisp leaves, torn or cut into bite-sized pieces or left whole if small, plus fresh herbs, seasonal vegetables or fruits, and such additions as olives or cheese. The all-important dressing marries the ingredients with its smooth consistency and complementary flavors.

When a salad is prepared with attention to detail, the results can be profoundly good. A green salad makes a fine impression when served at the start of a meal or, as some Europeans do, when offered as a palate refresher after the main course. Accompanied by good bread and a bowl of soup, it is a satisfying light meal in its own right.

The best green salads start with good ingredients. The guide on pages 9–14 surveys the many options for salad leaves and provides instructions on how to prepare them for the best results.

Spinach Salad with Grapefruit, Orange, and Avocado, 27

17

Tart Green Salad

4 to 6 servings

Follow the advice in Dressing Salads, 15, *allowing about 2 cups assorted greens per person. Toss the salad (opposite) with just enough vinaigrette to coat the leaves lightly but thoroughly (½ to ¾ cup for 4 servings).*
Combine in a salad bowl:

2 bunches arugula, tough stems trimmed, washed, dried, and torn into bite-sized pieces

3 Belgian endives, washed, dried, cores removed, cut crosswise into 1½-inch-thick slices
1 small head radicchio, washed, dried, and torn into bite-sized pieces
Toss well to coat with:
½ to ¾ cup *Fresh Herb Vinaigrette*, 108
Serve immediately.

Green Salad

4 to 6 servings

The ultimate after-dinner salad. Many markets sell premixed greens, but for a more personalized salad, select an assortment of the freshest salad greens available. Combine greens with contrasting pungencies, textures, and appearances for the most interest.
Combine in a salad bowl:

2 large heads Boston or Bibb lettuce, washed, dried, and torn into bite-sized pieces

1 tablespoon chopped fresh parsley (optional)
1 tablespoon snipped fresh chives (optional)
Toss well to coat with:
½ to ¾ cup *Basic Vinaigrette*, 108, or one of the variations
Serve immediately.

Field Salad with Fresh Herbs

4 to 6 servings

The idea of using whole herbs as salad greens seems rather novel to us today, but it has a long and noble history.
Combine in a salad bowl:

1 cup fresh herb leaves (any combination of chervil, sage, tarragon, dill, basil, marjoram, flat-leaf parsley, and mint)

4 cups bite-sized pieces salad greens (any combination of curly endive, radicchio, watercress, mâche, dandelion greens, and arugula), washed and dried
Toss well to coat with:
⅓ to ½ cup *Basic Vinaigrette*, 108
Serve immediately.

Garnished Green Salads

A green salad is easily transformed into an enticing appetizer or even a main course with the addition of a few ingredients chosen for texture, taste, and visual appeal. The greens remain dominant in these salads, so avoid the temptation to overwhelm them with too many bits of this and that. Think in terms of balance and harmony. Too many assertive garnishes, such as olives, garlic, and crumbled bacon, will cancel each other out. On the other hand, too many sweet flavors—fruit, soft cheese, carrots, and tomatoes—may become cloying. Begin by tasting the greens. If they are strong and pungent, they can support more flavor; mild and tender greens tolerate less.

The simplest way to enhance a green salad is to add condiments or seasonings to the salad while or after you toss it with the dressing. Be sure to give the greens a few extra tosses to integrate the additions well. With a light coat of dressing on the greens, small accents such as croutons, nuts, cheese, and olives will cling to the salad and are less apt to fall to the bottom of the bowl. For more substantial additions like grilled chicken, sliced beef, or the multiple ingredients of a Greek salad, everything gets tossed together at once. Following are some popular additions:

Tomatoes: There are those who say that it is unwise to add cut-up tomatoes to a tossed salad, as their juices will thin the dressing. If this possibility concerns you, prepare them separately and use them to garnish the salad bowl or cut the tomatoes into vertical slices instead of horizontal rounds, since they bleed less this way. Cherry tomatoes can be left whole. Even cut in half, they release little juice.

Croutons: Croutons are valued as much for their crunchy texture as for their flavor. Add these at the very last minute to prevent them from becoming soggy and leave them out if the salad is served alongside a starchy meal, such as pasta or rice.

Nuts and Seeds: Nuts and seeds add crunch and can complement the greens and the dressing. Simply place them in a dry skillet over medium heat and cook, stirring or shaking the pan often to prevent burning, until they begin to release their fragrance, about 4 minutes.

Vegetables: Thinly slice, shred, grate, or julienne raw vegetables such as carrots, cabbage, celery, cucumbers, bell peppers, fennel, and mushrooms so that they mix with the greens and do not fall like dead weight to the bottom of the bowl.

Garlic: Garlic is perhaps the most influential seasoning. There are two ways of giving a salad a delicate touch of this pungent flavor. Halve a clove of garlic, rub the inside of a salad bowl with the cut sides, then discard the clove. Or rub a rather dry crust of bread on all sides with a halved clove of garlic (this is called a *chapon*) and place it in the salad bowl under the greens. Add the dressing and toss the salad lightly to distribute the flavor; remove the *chapon* and serve the salad at once. The *chapon* itself can be served to a garlic enthusiast. For a slightly stronger flavor, mash a clove of garlic at the bottom of the salad bowl with the other seasonings and add the dressing to the bowl before the greens.

IDEAS FOR SALAD GARNISHES

Avocados, sliced

Bacon, crumbled

Cheese, sliced or crumbled

Chickpeas, kidney beans, or other cooked legumes

Fresh herbs

Hard-boiled eggs, chopped

Ham or other cured meats, thinly sliced

Smoked or cured fish (salmon, trout, mackerel), flaked

Marinated artichoke hearts, whole or sliced

Olives, pitted

Orange or grapefruit slices, peel and pith removed

Dried fruit (raisins, currants, cranberries, cherries)

Apples, sliced

Mangoes, sliced

Pears, sliced

Mixed Greens with Cheese Crisp

4 servings

Toss together in a small bowl:

½ cup grated Gruyère cheese

1 tablespoon grated Parmesan cheese

Sprinkle in an even layer in a large nonstick skillet to form an 8-inch disk. Cook over medium heat, spooning off the fat, until lightly browned, about 4 minutes. Using a spatula, carefully lift the pancake onto a paper–towel–lined baking sheet and blot dry.

Place in a salad bowl:

6 cups bite-sized pieces greens (romaine or Boston lettuce, or escarole), washed and dried

Toss the greens well to coat with:

⅓ to ½ cup *Basic Vinaigrette*, 108

Divide among 4 salad plates and crumble the cheese crisp on top.

Baby Asian Greens and Whole Herbs

4 to 6 servings

Most Asian greens have a pleasant edge that makes them a perfect accompaniment to rich meats (like lamb and beef) and fish (tuna, mackerel). Here we follow the Southeast Asian practice of combining greens with whole leaves of the herb trio of cilantro, mint, and basil. The herbs not only lend the salad additional flavor intensity but also add a kind of sweetness to balance the slightly bitter greens.

Bring to a boil in a small saucepan over high heat:

2 stalks lemongrass, coarsely chopped

2 tablespoons minced peeled fresh ginger

⅔ cup white vinegar

⅔ cup water

3 tablespoons sugar

Reduce the heat to low and simmer, uncovered, for 20 minutes, stirring occasionally. Strain and discard the solids. Add and whisk together:

2 tablespoons toasted sesame oil

2 tablespoons vegetable oil

2 tablespoons soy sauce

2 tablespoons fish sauce or vegetable oil

Combine in a salad bowl:

10 to 12 cups bite-sized pieces baby Asian greens (any combination of mizuna, tatsoi, baby mustard greens, komatsuna, baby bok choy, pea shoots, and baby shungiku), washed and dried

2 red bell peppers, cut into thin strips

½ cup cilantro leaves

¼ cup mint leaves

¼ cup basil leaves

Stir the dressing well, add just enough to moisten the salad, toss gently to coat, and serve.

Caesar Salad

6 servings

Whether to include anchovies in the salad was once the main point of discussion. Today the question is whether to top the Caesar with chicken breast, shrimp, or sliced beef. Any of these makes a fine addition, turning a first course into an entrée, but we retain an affection for the pure and genuine article. First coddling, or gently boiling, the egg helps to thicken the dressing.

Preheat the oven to 350°F.

Heat in a small saucepan over medium heat until the butter is melted:

2 tablespoons butter
2 tablespoons extra-virgin olive oil
2 cloves garlic, halved lengthwise
Salt and ground black pepper
    to taste

Remove from the heat and let stand for 10 minutes. Discard the garlic.

Toss with the butter mixture:

3 cups ½-inch cubes French or
    Italian bread

Spread on a baking sheet and bake, shaking the pan once or twice, until golden brown, 12 to 15 minutes.

Mash together in a small bowl until a paste is formed:

4 cloves garlic, peeled
½ teaspoon salt

Whisk in:

2 teaspoons fresh lemon juice
1 teaspoon Worcestershire sauce
Salt and ground black pepper
    to taste
2 to 4 anchovy fillets, rinsed,
    patted dry, and mashed to a
    paste (optional)

Add in a slow, steady stream, whisking constantly:

½ cup extra-virgin olive oil

In a salad bowl, toss the croutons and dressing with:

2 small heads romaine lettuce
    (preferably young or inner pale
    green leaves), washed, dried, and
    torn into bite-sized pieces
2 large eggs, boiled gently for
    2 minutes, or added raw (see *Egg*
    ***Safety, opposite*)**

Sprinkle with:

½ cup Parmesan cheese shavings

Serve immediately.

WESTERN SALAD

Prepare *Caesar Salad, left,* adding about ½ cup crumbled blue cheese, and omitting the anchovies.

Reduced-Fat Caesar Salad

6 servings

This is a reasonable stand-in for the classic Caesar for those who are concerned about fat intake.

Preheat the oven to 350°F.

Toss to combine well:

3 cups ½-inch cubes sourdough bread

5 spritzes olive oil spray

2 cloves garlic, finely minced

Salt and ground black pepper to taste

Spread on a baking sheet and bake, shaking the pan once or twice, until golden brown, about 10 minutes. Let cool.

Mash together in a small bowl until a paste is formed:

1 clove garlic, peeled

Pinch of salt

Whisk in:

2 tablespoons chicken stock

1 tablespoon grated Parmesan cheese

1 tablespoon minced fresh parsley

2 teaspoons sherry vinegar

1 teaspoon Dijon mustard

1 teaspoon fresh thyme leaves

2 anchovy fillets, rinsed, patted dry, and mashed to a paste (optional)

Add in a slow, steady stream, whisking constantly:

2 tablespoons extra-virgin olive oil

In a salad bowl, toss the croutons and dressing with:

2 small heads romaine lettuce (preferably young or inner pale green leaves), washed, dried, and torn into bite-sized pieces

3 tablespoons grated Parmesan cheese

Salt and ground black pepper to taste

Sprinkle with:

1 tablespoon grated Parmesan cheese

Serve immediately.

EGG SAFETY

The bacteria *Salmonella enteritidis*, which can cause illness and even death, is occasionally found in raw eggs, even uncracked eggs. Of great concern to some are a number of classic recipes that depend on raw or only lightly cooked eggs—among them Caesar salad and mayonnaise. Some cooks now substitute pasteurized liquid eggs (available both whole and separated). The liquid eggs most closely resemble fresh eggs and are only slightly less efficient than fresh eggs for emulsifying or whipping purposes. Some cooks refuse to compromise and continue using fresh eggs, raw or lightly cooked, without incident. If you are of this school, minimize risk by using the freshest eggs possible and storing them at temperatures below 40°F. You can also gently boil eggs in their shells for 2 minutes before using them in salads and dressings. Serve egg dishes immediately or refrigerate.

Greek Salad

4 to 6 servings

A good Greek salad should be more of a spontaneous event than an ironclad recipe. Feel free to add, omit, and substitute ingredients as whim or necessity dictates.

Combine in a salad bowl:

2 large or 3 small heads Boston, romaine, or iceberg lettuce, washed, dried, and torn into bite-sized pieces

8 cherry tomatoes or tomato wedges

½ cup coarsely crumbled feta cheese

6 thin slices red onion

½ cucumber, peeled and sliced

8 Kalamata olives, pitted

¾ cup diagonally sliced celery hearts

4 scallions, cut into 1-inch pieces

8 firm radishes, sliced

One 2-ounce can anchovy fillets, rinsed, patted dry, and halved lengthwise

Whisk together:

6 to 7 tablespoons olive oil

2 tablespoons fresh lemon juice or red wine vinegar

1 teaspoon finely minced garlic

1 teaspoon dried oregano

Salt and ground black pepper to taste

Pour the dressing over the salad and toss well. Serve immediately on chilled large plates.

ANCHOVIES

Anchovies, available worldwide, have a soft, delicate texture, a rather strong flavor, and dark-colored flesh. They are sold fresh (often confused with sardines and herring), packed in salt, and packed in oil. When fresh, anchovies need to be deboned like sardines. When they are packed in salt, you'll need to rinse and pick over them; when they are in oil, rinse if you wish and reserve the oil for use in cooking. Salted or canned anchovies are used as flavoring in salads; fresh anchovies can be grilled with excellent results. Despite their strong flavor, fresh anchovies are moderate to low in fat.

OLIVES

In the Mediterranean region, where most olives are grown, as much care is put into olive growing as into wine or cheese making. There is a wealth of piquant, nutty, sweet, and fruity olives available. From Greece, the famous Kalamata olives (opposite) are purple-black or maroon with a slender oval shape, soft texture, and rich flavor. California also produces some fine olives. Try bottled Californian Greek-style black or green olives and dry-cured black olives, which are quite meaty and tender. Buy olives that are uniform in color and free of surface blemishes. Keep loose olives in the refrigerator for several weeks; canned or bottled olives can be kept unopened on the shelf for up to two years and when opened should be refrigerated.

Spinach Salad

4 servings

Tender young spinach leaves are ideal for this classic salad. Young mustard greens or young dandelion leaves make delicious substitutes.

Cook in a skillet over medium-high heat until crisp:

4 slices bacon

Drain on paper towels and crumble. Combine well:

¼ cup cider vinegar or vinegar of your choice

2 tablespoons olive or vegetable oil

2 teaspoons yellow mustard seeds (optional)

2 teaspoons minced fresh parsley, or a combination of other fresh herbs

1 teaspoon grated onion

1 teaspoon sugar

Place in a salad bowl:

1 large bunch young spinach, trimmed, washed, and dried

Pour the dressing over the spinach and toss well. Sprinkle with the crumbled bacon and garnish with:

2 or 3 *Hard-Boiled Eggs*, 84, sliced into rounds

Serve immediately.

WARM SPINACH SALAD

Hard-boiled eggs take 12 to 15 minutes to become firm throughout, with a yolk that remains bright yellow. Prepare *Spinach Salad, left*, substituting 2 tablespoons of the bacon drippings for the oil if desired. Heat the dressing until just before it begins to boil and pour over the spinach greens. Garnish with the crumbled bacon and sliced hard-boiled eggs and serve immediately.

Baked Goat Cheese and Baby Greens

4 servings

In Provence, France, where this salad is popular, mesclun includes many different salad greens and herbs, each varying in flavor, texture, and color. A mix might contain red- and green-tipped oakleaf lettuce, arugula, romaine lettuce, chervil, colorful red radicchio, and curly white as well as green endive, escarole, and bitter dandelion greens. Add fresh herbs to this mixture (sage, dill, and tarragon are our favorites), top with baked goat cheese, and you have a delicious lunch or supper dish.

Preheat the oven to 400°F. Grease a small baking dish.
Refrigerate in a salad bowl:

6 cups mixed baby greens or mesclun, washed and dried

Stir together in a shallow bowl:

1 cup fine dry unseasoned breadcrumbs

1 teaspoon dried thyme

Pour into another shallow bowl:

¼ cup extra-virgin olive oil

Coat first with the olive oil and then with the breadcrumbs:

4 rounds fresh goat cheese, each about 2½ inches in diameter and ½ inch thick

Place the cheese on the baking dish and bake until golden brown and lightly bubbling, about 6 minutes. Meanwhile, prepare:

Basic Vinaigrette, 108

Toss the greens with just enough vinaigrette to coat and divide among 4 salad plates. Place a round of baked cheese in the center of each salad and serve at once.

Spinach Salad with Grapefruit, Orange, and Avocado

2 to 4 servings

Toast briefly in a small skillet over medium heat:

3 tablespoons sesame seeds

Toss together in a salad bowl:

3 generous handfuls (about 6 cups) baby spinach leaves, washed and dried

2 to 3 pinches of salt

3 to 4 tablespoons *Tangerine Shallot Dressing*, 113

Divide the spinach among chilled salad plates and arrange evenly over the greens:

1 grapefruit, peeled and sectioned

1 navel orange, peeled and sectioned

1 ripe avocado, peeled and sliced

Sprinkle with the sesame seeds and season with:

Ground black pepper to taste

Serve immediately.

WARM OR WILTED SALADS

In the classic *Warm Spinach Salad, opposite*, a hot dressing partially cooks the greens, rendering them succulent and tender. In others, a warm garnish, such as baked goat cheese or fresh tuna hot off the grill, is placed on a bed of cool, crisp greens, producing a dramatic contrast of temperature and texture. These salads make an impressive first course or a memorable entrée. Keep in mind that whatever your choice, you should always serve warm salads immediately, because they lose their appeal as the greens become soggy.

Endive and Walnut Salad

4 servings

Whisk together in a salad bowl:

1 tablespoon red wine vinegar
1 tablespoon minced shallots
½ teaspoon Dijon mustard
**Salt and ground black pepper
to taste**

Add in a slow, steady stream, whisking constantly:

2 tablespoons walnut oil

2 tablespoons vegetable oil
Add:
**8 Belgian endives, washed, dried,
cores removed, cut crosswise
into ½-inch-thick slices**
½ cup walnut halves, toasted
**¼ cup crumbled Gorgonzola or
other blue cheese (optional)**
Toss well to coat. Serve immediately.

Romaine and Red Onion Salad with Corn Bread Croutons

4 servings

*Croutons made from good rye or
whole-wheat herb bread can be substituted for ones made with corn bread.
Cut ½-inch-thick slices from a whole
loaf, then cut into ½-inch cubes.*
Preheat the oven to 350°F.
Toss together on a baking sheet:

**2 cups ½-inch cubes corn bread
(about 2 large pieces)**
2 tablespoons extra-virgin olive oil
Bake, shaking the pan once or twice,
until golden, about 10 minutes.
Transfer to a salad bowl and let cool.
Whisk together in a small bowl:

2 cloves garlic, minced
**2 tablespoons grated Parmesan
cheese**
2 tablespoons balsamic vinegar
2 tablespoons chicken stock
**1 teaspoon chopped fresh basil or
parsley, or to taste**
**Salt and ground black pepper
to taste**
Add in a slow, steady stream, whisking constantly:
¼ cup olive oil
In a salad bowl, combine:

**2 small heads romaine lettuce,
washed, dried, and torn into
bite-sized pieces**
1 small red onion, thinly sliced
Add the dressing and toss to coat
the greens. Add the croutons and
combine. Sprinkle with:
Parmesan cheese shavings
Serve immediately.

CROUTONS

These dried or fried seasoned fresh
bread morsels come in all sizes.
These are made by cutting bread,
preferably simple French bread,
into small or large dice or square
slices, buttering them or rubbing
them with olive oil, and toasting
in a 375°F oven until crisp, 10 to
15 minutes. Oil-free croutons can
be made by cutting up bread into
small cubes and slowly drying
them at 200°F. These are perfect
for stuffings and poultry dressings.

Arugula with Summer Vegetables

4 to 6 servings

Use this recipe as a rough guideline, substituting whatever summer vegetables are most plentiful in the market. Baby turnip or beet greens or Swiss chard leaves can be substituted for the mâche and/or arugula.

Prepare:

Basic Vinaigrette, 108, or one of the variations

Cook in a large pot of boiling water for about 1 minute:

1 small summer squash, cut into ½-inch cubes, or 6 pattypan squash, cut in half

Remove with a large slotted spoon, refresh in ice water, and drain well. Add to the boiling water:

8 ounces thin green beans, trimmed

Cook just until crisp-tender, about 1 minute. Remove with a large slotted spoon, refresh in ice water, and drain well. Combine the squash and green beans in a salad bowl along with:

2 cups cherry tomatoes, halved

1 small red onion, halved and very thinly sliced

⅓ cup minced fresh basil

Toss well with enough of the vinaigrette to coat. Taste and adjust the seasonings. Divide among salad plates:

4 cups bite-sized pieces arugula and romaine lettuce, washed and dried

Spoon the vegetables on top. Drizzle more dressing over the salads and garnish with:

Fresh basil leaves (optional)

Serve immediately.

ABOUT
VEGETABLE &
SAVORY FRUIT
SALADS

*N*owadays vegetable salads and savory fruit salads attractively arranged and dressed are a much-appreciated alternative to green salads. The variety of textures and tastes in vegetables and fruits gives these salads a greater range of possibilities than their leafy cousins. Whatever the recipe, select produce at the peak of freshness, for there is no hiding inferior ingredients in these pure and simple creations. Vegetable salads are made from raw or cooked vegetables, solo or combined with others. Fruits are left uncooked and sometimes mixed with other fruits and vegetables. Do not limit yourself to just the recipes on these pages, delicious though they may be. Almost any vegetable makes an interesting and often elegant salad when steamed or blanched and paired with a dressing. Try combining green beans, snap peas, artichokes, asparagus, or leeks with Spicy Walnut Vinaigrette, 110, or Tangerine Shallot Dressing, 113, or any of the vinaigrettes on pages 108–111. Serve these salads to spark the appetite before a meal, as a refreshing side dish, or include several on a buffet table.

Classic Cole Slaw, 48

31

Avocados

Grown in southern California and Florida, avocados are available year-round. California specializes in the Hass, a purplish black, pebbly skinned avocado of the Guatemalan type. Hass avocados weigh about 8 ounces. Their flesh is so rich and buttery because it contains twice as much fat as the smaller, smooth-skinned, green Mexican type of avocados that are grown in Florida. (California's other avocado, smooth green Fuerte, is probably a Guatemalan-Mexican hybrid.) Although fat means calories, most fat in avocados is mono-unsaturated, the friendly sort found in olives. From southern Florida

and Hawaii also comes the yellow-skinned West Indian avocado. Should you find 1- to 2-ounce cocktail avocados (they are Fuertes or Mexican fruits with no seed, remnants of dropped pollinated flowers), prepare as usual.

Choose an unblemished fruit that is heavy for its size, ideally one that is tender when gently pressed between your hands. Ripe avocados are rare at the market, so plan to buy them about 3 days before you will need them. Until it is cut, a stone-hard avocado will ripen by the paper bag method. Place underripe avocados in a brown paper bag, making

sure not to crowd them. Place the bag at room temperature out of the sun. Turn the bag over every day so the avocados ripen evenly. Adding an apple or banana will speed the process because these fruits emit a harmless gas that enhances ripening.

Slightly overripe fruit can be used for mashing but not slicing. Refrigerate ripe fruits for up to 2 days.

Avocado flesh quickly darkens when exposed to air. This does not affect quality or flavor but mars the beauty of the fruit. To prevent darkening, immediately rub cut surfaces with a slice of citrus.

HOW TO PIT AND PEEL AVOCADOS

Pitting and peeling an avocado requires nothing more than a sharp heavy knife and a little attention. While a perfectly ripe avocado practically pits and peels itself, an unripe avocado will cling to its pit (and makes for unrewarding eating) and an overripe avocado will disintegrate into mush rather than be neatly sliced. See above for ripening avocados using the paper bag method.

1 With a sharp heavy knife, cut a ripe avocado lengthwise in half (through the stem end) by drawing the blade of the knife around the large central pit.

2 Gently twist the halves apart. If the avocado is ripe, the two halves will come apart easily. If not fully ripe, some flesh might stick to the pit. The pit will be lodged in one of the halves.

3 Tap the large pit with the blade of the knife with enough force to imbed the knife in the pit. Give the handle of the knife a twist to free the pit, then lift it out. Grasp the pit with a paper towel in one hand and carefully pull the knife free from the pit with the other hand. You can scoop out the flesh, or peel the skin away.

Avocado Slices

4 to 6 servings

The soft, buttery texture and taste of avocados combine beautifully with the sharp, tangy flavors of citrus and vinaigrettes. Serve lightly dressed avocado slices as a garnish for grilled meats and fish or arrange them on a bed of crisp lettuce as a sprightly first course. Select only ripe fruit.

Cut crosswise on a slight angle into ¼-inch-thick slices:

2 ripe avocados, chilled and peeled
Marinate for 5 minutes in:
½ to ¾ cup Basic Vinaigrette, 108, or one of the variations
Arrange the slices in an overlapping fan shape on a bed of lettuce.
Sprinkle with:
Chopped fresh parsley, chives, or mint
Serve immediately.

AVOCADO AND CITRUS SALAD

For this salad, choose citrus fruits that are heavy for their size (above). Prepare Avocado Slices, left, alternating the avocados with sections of grapefruit and orange that have been trimmed of peel, pith, and membrane.

Tunisian-Style Carrot Salad

4 appetizer servings

To add extra bite to this salad (opposite), stir in 2 diced radishes just before serving.

Peel and coarsely grate into a large bowl:

4 medium carrots

Add:

2 red bell peppers, cut into thin matchsticks

12 Kalamata or other olives, pitted and quartered

Mix well:

½ cup orange juice

2 tablespoons olive oil

1 tablespoon fresh lemon juice

1 teaspoon ground coriander

1 teaspoon ground cumin

¼ teaspoon ground cinnamon

¼ teaspoon red pepper flakes, or to taste

Salt and ground black pepper to taste

Add to the carrot mixture, toss well, and serve, accompanied, if desired, with:

Grilled pita wedges

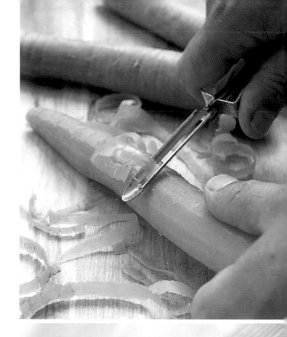

Carrot and Raisin Salad

4 servings

If you have the time, crisp the peeled carrots on ice for an hour before grating.

Combine in a medium bowl:

4 large carrots, peeled and coarsely grated

½ cup raisins

½ cup coarsely chopped pecans or unsalted roasted peanuts

2 teaspoons grated lemon zest

1 tablespoon fresh lemon juice

¾ teaspoon salt

Ground black pepper to taste

Pour over:

1 cup sour cream, or ½ cup sour cream and ½ cup mayonnaise

Toss well and serve.

Carrot, Apple, and Horseradish Salad

4 to 6 servings

To convert this into a reduced-fat salad, use low-fat or fat-free yogurt in place of the sour cream.

Stir together well in a bowl:

2 cups coarsely grated peeled carrots

2 large Granny Smith or other tart apples, peeled, cored, and coarsely grated

½ cup sour cream or low-fat or fat-free yogurt

2 to 3 tablespoons finely grated peeled fresh horseradish or drained bottled horseradish

2 tablespoons chopped fresh parsley

2 tablespoons snipped fresh chives

1 teaspoon fresh lemon juice

1 teaspoon sugar

Cover and refrigerate until the salad is cold, about 1 hour. Serve.

Tomato Salad

6 to 8 servings

It is hard to beat a salad of freshly harvested, juicy, ripe summer tomatoes dressed with a bit of good olive oil and vinegar and some parsley. Choose the best tomatoes you can find—fully ripe but not too soft. Combine red and yellow tomatoes for a colorful effect.

Arrange so that they overlap around or across a chilled platter:

6 large ripe tomatoes (preferably vine ripened), cut into ½-inch-thick slices or wedges

Drizzle over the tomatoes:

½ cup extra-virgin olive oil, or more to taste

Splash of balsamic vinegar

Sprinkle with:

¼ cup minced fresh parsley

Salt and ground black pepper to taste

Do not refrigerate. Serve immediately.

TOMATO SALAD VINAIGRETTE

Prepare *Tomato Salad, left,* substituting *Basic Vinaigrette, 108,* or any of the variations for the oil, vinegar, parsley, and seasonings.

TOMATO AND ONION SALAD

Prepare *Tomato Salad, left,* alternating thin slices of red onion with the tomato slices.

Tomato and Mozzarella Salad (Insalata Caprese)

4 to 6 servings

Named for the island of Capri, where it was perhaps first made, this gloriously simple salad is popular all over Italy and is increasingly so in the United States.

Arrange, alternating slices, on a platter:

4 large ripe tomatoes, cut into ½-inch-thick slices

12 ounces mozzarella cheese, cut into ¼-inch-thick slices

Sprinkle with:

1½ cups fresh basil leaves

Drizzle over the salad:

½ cup olive oil, preferably extra virgin

Salt to taste

Serve at once or let stand at room temperature for up to 1 hour before serving. In either case, do not refrigerate the salad.

TOMATO, GOAT CHEESE, AND BASIL SALAD

A light goat cheese works best in this tomato salad. We suggest a young Montrachet or a Bûcheron. Prepare *Tomato and Mozzarella Salad, left,* substituting 3 ounces fresh goat cheese, sliced ¼ inch thick, for the mozzarella.

Dee's Corn and Tomato Salad

4 servings

We were first served this wonderful expression of seasonal tastes by our friend Dee Schmid.

Cut the kernels from:

6 ears sweet white corn, briefly blanched and cooled

Combine in a bowl with:

1 large tomato, diced

½ red onion, diced

1 to 2 tablespoons chopped fresh basil

Barely moisten with:

Basic Vinaigrette, 108

Serve chilled or at room temperature within 2 to 3 hours, garnished with:

Fresh basil leaves

TOMATOES

Tomatoes come in many sizes but only two basic shapes: round and oval. Cherry tomatoes are usually the first round tomatoes in season. Their skins are relatively tough, but their flesh is sweet and juicy. They may be red, gold, orange, or yellow-green. South American currant tomatoes, the size and shape of currants, are the closest things to wild tomatoes that most of us will ever taste. Their flavor is ultrasweet, especially the yellow ones. Keep an eye out, too, for little grape tomatoes. These miniatures, no bigger than the fruit after which they are named, may be costlier than cherry tomatoes; but their consistently sweet and tangy flavor more than merits the expense.

Most standard-sized round tomatoes are as juicy as cherry tomatoes. Several sizes found in most farmers' markets offer an even greater variety, and home gardens can provide the best selection of all. Salad tomatoes are small to medium in size and tend to be moderately juicy. Large beefsteak tomatoes (one of the largest varieties) are usually served sliced. In season, they are meaty, rich, and juicy, not to mention dark and deep in color. Also look for so-called heritage or heirloom varieties of tomatoes, seasonal treats that come in a rainbow of colors and even patterns, with delightfully distinctive flavors to match.

Most tomatoes raised for mass commerce are picked green and continue to develop their red color off the vine. But since sugars cannot increase in a fruit after picking, their flavor will not improve with ripening. The finest commercial tomatoes will be labeled "vine-ripened." Although usually harvested not fully matured, they will have spent more time on the vine and will have begun to show their color at the time of picking.

Out of season, commercially raised tomatoes typically look like tomatoes and slice like tomatoes, but they lack the true taste of a garden-grown summer tomato, and with good reason. Most of them will have been grown in greenhouses or hydroponically— that is, in water rather than in soil.

Select firm, bright specimens that feel heavy for their size. Scarring around the stem end is harmless. Any stems or leaves still attached should look moist and fresh. If the tomato smells like a tomato, grab it. Home-grown tomatoes should be picked when they are fragrant. Whether you grow tomatoes in season yourself or buy peak-of-season tomatoes from local growers, eat them the same day they are picked if possible. If not, remember to store underripe to firm ripe tomatoes at room temperature, unwrapped. Store ripe tomatoes, those that yield to the touch, unwrapped on a refrigerator shelf, rather than in the moister environment of a vegetable crisper.

Pita Salad (Fattoush)

4 servings

This is a refreshing Syrian salad (opposite). If you are in a hurry, replace the cucumber with pieces of washed and dried romaine or cos lettuce.

Toss together in a colander:

1 small cucumber, peeled, seeded, and cut into ½-inch cubes

1 teaspoon salt

Let stand to drain for 30 minutes. Preheat the oven to 350°F.

Open on a baking sheet and bake until crisp and lightly browned, about 10 minutes:

Two 7-inch pita breads

Break into bite-sized pieces. Press the excess water out of the cucumbers, rinse quickly, and blot dry. Combine the cucumbers in a medium bowl with:

3 medium ripe tomatoes, chopped

1 small green bell pepper, diced (optional)

6 scallions, white and tender green parts, finely chopped

2 tablespoons chopped fresh cilantro

⅓ cup chopped fresh parsley

1 tablespoon finely chopped fresh mint

Whisk together in a small bowl:

⅓ cup olive oil, preferably extra virgin

Juice of 1 large lemon (about ¼ cup)

1 clove garlic, crushed

¼ teaspoon salt

Pour the dressing over the vegetables and toss well. Add the pita toasts, toss again, and serve immediately.

Bread and Tomato Salad (Panzanella)

8 to 10 servings

Traditionally, stale bread in Italy (and in many homes throughout the world) was never thrown away. It was grated into breadcrumbs and added to savory fillings or used as the basis for salads like this one. Here country-style Italian or French bread is lightly toasted to make it dry enough to soak up the dressing.

Preheat the oven to 350°F.

Spread on a baking sheet:

5 cups 1-inch bread cubes

Bake, shaking the pan once or twice, until browned, 10 to 15 minutes.

Whisk together in a small bowl until blended:

½ cup extra-virgin olive oil

½ cup red wine vinegar

¼ cup fresh lemon juice

¼ cup minced fresh parsley

1 teaspoon minced garlic

Salt and cracked black peppercorns to taste

In a salad bowl, toss the croutons and dressing with:

3 cucumbers, peeled, seeded, and cut into ½-inch cubes

3 large ripe tomatoes, cut into ½-inch cubes

1 large red onion, cut into ½-inch cubes

½ cup pitted Kalamata or other brine-cured black olives

½ cup fresh basil leaves

Add the dressing, toss well, and remove to a large platter. Sprinkle with:

½ cup Parmesan cheese shavings

Serve at once.

Cucumber and Yogurt Salad

4 to 6 servings

This salad is based on tzatziki, *the Greek cucumber and yogurt sauce.*
Set a very fine mesh sieve or a colander lined with a coffee filter or several layers of cheesecloth over a bowl. Add and let drain at room temperature for at least 2 hours or in the refrigerator for up to 24 hours:

2 cups yogurt

Toss together in a colander:

1 large cucumber, peeled, seeded, and diced

1 teaspoon salt

Let stand to drain for 30 minutes. Press the excess water out of the cucumbers, rinse quickly, and blot dry. Mash together until a paste is formed:

2 cloves garlic, peeled

2 to 3 pinches of salt

Combine the yogurt, cucumbers, and garlic in a medium bowl along with:

2 to 3 teaspoons white wine vinegar

2 teaspoons chopped fresh mint

2 teaspoons snipped fresh dill

Salt and ground white pepper to taste

Drizzle over the salad (opposite):

1 tablespoon olive oil, preferably extra virgin

Cucumber Salad

4 servings

Combine in a small bowl:

¼ cup rice vinegar

4 teaspoons sesame seeds, toasted

2 teaspoons superfine sugar

Add and toss to coat:

1 large cucumber, scrubbed or peeled if waxed, halved crosswise, and cut into thin strips or thinly sliced crosswise

Cover and refrigerate until the salad is cold, about 1 hour. Serve.

CUCUMBERS

These quenching vegetables—about 96 percent water—are cucurbitas, part of a huge family that includes squashes. They may be field or hothouse grown, long and slender or stubby or round, and nearly seedless or filled with seeds. We eat them when they are green and immature. Be sure to select firm, hard cucumbers. Unless you are dealing with the roundish "apple" cucumber, yellowness is an undesirable trait, as is flabbiness. Both signify age, a pithy interior, and a tough skin. Otherwise, the skin is edible, sometimes even by allergic people who cannot tolerate the pulp alone. The skin should have a slight sheen; if highly polished, however, keep in mind that the cucumber has probably been waxed and should then be peeled. If you wish to make the cucumbers more decorative, you can leave them unpeeled and score them with a fork before slicing.

Potato Salad

The best potatoes for any salad are waxy, or low-starch, potatoes, as opposed to the starchy tubers known as russet, or baking, potatoes. Waxy potatoes hold their shape once cooked and will not crumble when sliced or diced. Red Bliss and Yellow Finn are popular varieties for salads. New potatoes are also favored because their thin skins do not need peeling.

Potato salad is best prepared from scrubbed potatoes cooked in their jackets just until soft enough to be easily pierced with a fork. Over-cooking destroys the potato's texture, while undercooking dampens the potato's flavor. The skins are easily removed after cooking if desired. Cut potatoes for salad into either large dice or thick slices as soon as they are cool enough to handle. Potatoes absorb the maximum flavor from a dressing when still warm; so with the exception of mayonnaise- or cream-based dressings, which can separate or spoil, toss just-cooked potatoes with the dressing and serve the salad either warm or after it has cooled to room temperature. For mayonnaise- and cream-based salads, allow the potatoes to cool slightly but *do not refrigerate them before you put the dressing on*, as they will lose much of their down-to-earth savor. In either case, toss potatoes gently to keep them intact.

HOW TO BOIL POTATOES

Potatoes containing relatively high moisture and low starch are described as waxy and are called boilers. *These are the potatoes that hold their shape as cubes and slices in potato salads. Select potatoes that are firm and heavy for their size, with taut skin and no cuts, dark spots, cracks, mold, or other sign of spoilage. If there is a greenish cast to the potato or a green patch on it, avoid it—the green part was exposed to the sun and will be bitter (even mildly toxic). Avoid those potatoes that have sprouted.*

Leave skins on whenever possible— the skin is valuable nutritionally and packs a great amount of a potato's earthy flavor. Scrub the potatoes with a fairly stiff vegetable brush. If it is essential to peel, use a swivel peeler. Flesh exposed to air will darken if not cooked soon, so work quickly or drop pieces in a bowl of cold water mixed with a few drops of lemon juice or vinegar. It is best not to keep vegetables in water for more than 20 minutes, lest nutrients and flavor start leaching out.

1 Place 1 or 2 pounds potatoes in a large pot and add enough cold water to cover by 1 inch. Add 1 teaspoon salt for each quart of water.

2 Bring the potatoes to a boil and cook until tender when pierced with a thin skewer. You can also use the tip of a knife. Allow 10 to 15 minutes for whole small or baby potatoes, 20 to 25 minutes for medium, and 35 to 45 minutes for whole large potatoes. Slices ¼ inch thick will cook in 5 to 7 minutes.

American Potato Salad

6 to 8 servings

Many cooks customize their potato salad with such additions as hard-boiled eggs, sweet pickle relish, black olives, crumbled crisp cooked bacon, mint, pimientos, whole-grain mustard, or halved cherry tomatoes—not all of these at once, of course.

Bring to a boil in a large pot with enough salted cold water to cover by 1 inch:

2 pounds red or other waxy potatoes

Reduce the heat and simmer, uncovered, until the potatoes are tender when pierced with a fork, 20 to 25 minutes. Drain, peel if desired, and cut into bite-sized pieces. In a medium bowl, toss the still-warm potatoes with:

1 medium celery stalk, diced
2 tablespoons finely snipped fresh chives, or 2 scallions, minced, or 2 tablespoons minced red onion
¼ cup minced fresh parsley

Stir together:

¾ to 1 cup mayonnaise
2 tablespoons milk or red wine vinegar

Add the mayonnaise mixture to the warm potato mixture and toss gently to coat. Season with:

Salt and ground black pepper to taste

Serve at room temperature or chilled.

German Potato Salad

6 servings

German potato salad is traditionally served warm or even hot, but leftovers are good cold as well.

Place in a medium bowl while still warm:

2 pounds red or other waxy potatoes, prepared as directed for *American Potato Salad*, 43

Cook in a skillet over medium heat until crisp, 6 to 8 minutes:

4 slices bacon

Place the bacon on paper towels to drain, crumble it, and add it to the potatoes. Pour all but 2 tablespoons of the bacon fat out of the pan. Cook in the remaining fat over medium heat until golden, about 4 minutes:

1 small onion, diced
1 cup chopped celery with leaves (optional)

Add:

1 dill pickle, chopped (optional)

Add and bring just to a boil:

½ cup chicken stock, beef stock, or water

¼ cup white wine vinegar or cider vinegar
1 teaspoon sugar
1 teaspoon sweet paprika
1 teaspoon dry mustard (optional)
Salt and ground black pepper to taste

Pour the dressing over the potatoes, toss gently to coat, and garnish with:

Chopped fresh parsley and/or snipped fresh chives

Serve immediately.

French Potato Salad

6 to 8 servings

Place in a medium bowl while still warm:

2 pounds red or other waxy potatoes, prepared as directed for *American Potato Salad*, 43

Whisk together in a small bowl:

6 tablespoons red or white wine vinegar, or ¼ cup white wine vinegar and 2 tablespoons dry white wine

1 shallot, minced, or ½ red onion, minced, or 3 tablespoons finely snipped fresh chives
2 tablespoons minced fresh parsley
2 tablespoons drained capers (optional)
1 tablespoon whole-grain mustard
1 tablespoon minced fresh tarragon, mint, dill, or thyme (optional)

Salt and ground black pepper to taste

Add in a slow, steady stream, whisking constantly:

6 tablespoons olive oil

Pour the dressing over the potatoes, toss gently to combine, and serve warm, at room temperature, or chilled.

CAPERS

These are the preserved buds of a white flower on a spiny Mediterranean shrub. Freshly picked, the buds are startlingly bitter, reminiscent of raw artichoke hearts. The smallest capers are called nonpareil. Capers are far better packed under salt but are usually found in brine. Always drain and rinse capers before using, however they are packed. Chopped gherkins can be used in place of capers.

Tzatziki Potato Salad

6 servings

Tzatziki, a Greek yogurt sauce, makes a superb and unexpected dressing, low in fat but high in flavor.

Set a very fine mesh sieve or a colander lined with a coffee filter or several layers of cheesecloth over a bowl. Add and let drain at room temperature for at least 2 hours or, covered, in the refrigerator for up to 24 hours:

2 cups low-fat yogurt

Meanwhile, toss together in a colander set over a bowl and let drain at room temperature for at least 1 hour or, covered, in the refrigerator for up to 24 hours:

1 cucumber, scrubbed or peeled if waxed, seeded, and finely diced

1 teaspoon salt

Squeeze the cucumber in a dish towel to remove as much liquid as possible, then dry completely on paper towels. Combine the yogurt and cucumber in a large bowl along with:

2 tablespoons extra-virgin olive oil

1 tablespoon finely snipped fresh dill

1 tablespoon minced fresh mint

1 tablespoon red wine vinegar, or more to taste

Ground black pepper to taste

Mash together until a paste is formed:

2 cloves garlic, peeled

½ teaspoon salt

Stir into the yogurt mixture. Let stand for 1 hour or refrigerate, covered, for up to 24 hours. Meanwhile, place in a medium bowl while still warm and let cool to room temperature:

2 pounds red or other waxy potatoes, prepared as directed for *American Potato Salad*, 43

Salt and ground black pepper to taste

Add the tzatziki and toss gently to coat evenly. Cover and refrigerate. Serve chilled or at cool room temperature, garnished with:

Thin cucumber slices

Fresh dill sprigs

Fresh mint sprigs

Creamy Beet Salad

4 to 6 servings

Toss the salad while the beets are still warm so that they thoroughly absorb the dressing. The recipe can be prepared 3 to 4 hours in advance.
Cut into ¾-inch cubes and place in a medium bowl:
4 medium beets (about 1½ pounds), cooked and peeled

Whisk together in a small bowl:
2 teaspoons red wine vinegar
Salt to taste
Gradually whisk in until well blended:
2 tablespoons olive oil
1 tablespoon vegetable oil
Stir in:

2 tablespoons heavy cream
1 tablespoon drained horseradish
Ground white pepper to taste
Pour the dressing over the beets and toss to coat evenly. Garnish with:
Snipped fresh dill (optional)

BEETS

A source of sugar, beets are an intensely sweet vegetable, but a trace of sharpness keeps their flavor from being cloying. Once there was just the crimson beet, but now beets are also gold, orange, white, and candy striped; they can be perfectly round or long and slender, no bigger than the tip of your thumb or as big as your fist. Beets are available most of the year but are best from summer through early winter. When selecting a bunch of beets, if all the roots are equally fine, choose the bunch with the smallest leaves that are in the best condition (not yellowing or tattered). The greens are an indication of freshness for the roots; if they look moist and fresh, the roots will be too. If you are buying beets without leaves, be sure to avoid any that look dry, cracked, or shriveled.

Beets go especially well with lemon and orange, vinegar, any form of cream, onions, walnuts, parsley, caraway seeds, dill, tarragon, and mustard. Allow about 5 ounces of beets per serving.

In cooking, both roots and leaves bleed their colors into any dish they are in—except for golden beets, which hold their color. When handling cooked red beets, you may want to wear rubber gloves, as red beet juice can stain the hands for hours. Cooked beets are wonderful hot or cold. Serve small beets whole; slice larger ones into sections or rounds. Young, tender beets are delightful grated raw into a salad. Beets of any size are delicious steamed, baked, and microwaved.

HOW TO COOK AND PEEL BEETS

1 Cut off the leaves, leaving 1 to 2 inches of the stem, and keep the rootlets, or tails, in place.

2 Scrub beets well just before cooking but do not remove the skin.

Cook by one of the following methods. **To Boil:** For every 1 pound prepared beets, bring 12 cups water and 1½ tablespoons salt to a boil in a stockpot. Add the beets, rapidly return the water to a boil, then cook, covered, until tender when pierced through with a thin skewer. Allow about 20 minutes for small and baby beets, 30 to 35 minutes for medium, and 45 to 60 minutes for large beets. Drain, then plunge into cold water to cool. **To Steam:** Arrange the prepared beets in a single layer in a steaming basket over 1 to 2 inches boiling water. Cover and steam until tender when pierced through with a thin skewer, 25 to 30 minutes for small and baby beets, 35 to 40 minutes for medium, and up to 60 minutes for large beets. Add boiling water to the steamer as needed. **To Microwave:** Place 5 medium unpeeled beets in a 2-quart baking dish. Add ¼ cup stock or lightly salted water. Cover and cook on high until tender when pierced with a thin skewer, 12 to 18 minutes, stirring every 5 minutes. Let stand, still covered, for 3 minutes.

3 When cool enough to handle, slice off the stems and rootlets and slip off the skins.

Roasted Potatoes, Beets, and Onions Vinaigrette

6 servings

Preheat the oven to 375°F. Toss together and arrange in a single layer in a roasting pan:

12 fingerling or creamer potatoes, halved or quartered lengthwise
12 cloves garlic
2 tablespoons olive oil
Fresh rosemary or thyme sprigs
Salt and ground black pepper

Toss together and arrange in another roasting pan:

8 ounces cipolline or pearl onions, peeled

1 tablespoon olive oil
Salt and ground black pepper

Toss together and arrange in a third roasting pan:

¾ pound baby red, chiogga, or golden beets, stemmed and scrubbed
1 tablespoon olive oil
Salt and ground black pepper

Tightly cover each pan with foil and roast the vegetables until tender, 35 to 40 minutes; uncover potatoes and garlic after 20 minutes to allow them to brown and crisp slightly. Reserve any juices from the beets and onions and stir into:

Basic Vinaigrette, **108, preferably made with balsamic vinegar**

While the beets are still warm, gently rub their skins off using paper towels. Arrange the roasted vegetables around a mound of:

1 cup loosely packed mixed fresh herb leaves

Drizzle the vinaigrette over the salad. Serve at room temperature.

Cole Slaw

There are probably as many versions of cole slaw as there are people who make it. The one constant is raw cabbage (the name itself comes from the Dutch *koolsla*, meaning "cabbage salad"). After that, all bets are off. The cabbage may be red, white, or green; the dressing may be vinaigrette or have a base of mayonnaise or sour cream; and the salad may contain a vast array of other ingredients, among them bacon, carrots, bell peppers, pineapple, pickles, onions, and herbs.

To prepare the cabbage, remove any wilted leaves, then rinse. To cut, use a large, heavy knife to halve or quarter the cabbage through the stem. Cut around the core and remove it. Slice the halves or quarters into thin shreds. Soaking the shredded cabbage in ice-cold water for an hour before draining and dressing renders it refreshingly crisp.

Classic Cole Slaw

6 servings

For creamy slaw, stir together until well blended:

¾ cup *Traditional Mayonnaise*, 116, or Blender Mayonnaise, 118
¼ cup white vinegar
1 tablespoon sugar

For tart slaw, prepare:

½ to 1 cup *Basic Vinaigrette*, 108, other vinaigrette of your choice, 108 to 111, or Sour Cream Dressing for Vegetable Salads, 115

Finely shred or chop:

1 small head chilled green or red cabbage, cored and outer leaves removed

Stir in just enough of the dressing of your choice, creamy or tart, to moisten the cabbage. Season with:

Salt and ground black pepper to taste

If desired, add any of the following:

Crumbled crisp bacon
Dill, caraway, or celery seeds, or a combination
Chopped fresh parsley, chives, or other herb
Pineapple chunks
Grated peeled carrots
Coarsely chopped onions, bell peppers, or pickles

Stir again and serve immediately.

Asian Cole Slaw

4 to 6 servings

This is a cross between cole slaw and the Korean pickled, fermented cabbage staple called kimchee. *Letting the cabbage stand with salt draws out some of its moisture so that the salad remains crunchy.*

Toss together in a colander:

½ head green or red cabbage, cored and outer leaves removed, finely shredded
1 tablespoon salt

Place a plate on top of the cabbage and weight it with heavy cans or a bag of sugar or flour. Let the cabbage drain at room temperature for 3 hours.

Whisk together in a large bowl until the sugar is dissolved:

1 cup rice vinegar
1 cup sugar
2 tablespoons minced peeled fresh ginger
1 teaspoon red pepper flakes, or to taste

Rinse and drain the cabbage and dry it well. Add it to the vinegar mixture along with:

1 cup finely shredded peeled carrots

Toss well. Cover and refrigerate for at least 8 hours or up to 24 hours. Serve cold, garnished with:

Fresh cilantro leaves

Tangy Reduced-Fat Cole Slaw

4 servings

This cole slaw has less than 75 calories per serving and excellent flavor. Drained yogurt can be substituted for sour cream in almost any recipe.

Set a very fine mesh sieve or a colander lined with a coffee filter or several layers of cheesecloth over a bowl. Add and let drain at room temperature for at least 2 hours or, covered, in the refrigerator for up to 24 hours:

½ cup nonfat yogurt

Transfer the yogurt to a bowl. Add and whisk together until smooth:

1½ tablespoons cider vinegar
1 tablespoon sugar
1 tablespoon snipped fresh dill
1 teaspoon drained prepared horseradish
½ teaspoon dry mustard
Salt and ground black pepper to taste

Combine in a large bowl:

4 cups finely shredded green or red cabbage
1 cup grated peeled carrots

Add the dressing to the cabbage mixture and toss to coat evenly. Refrigerate, covered, for at least 1 hour. Serve chilled.

HORSERADISH

This long, cream-colored, tapering root is grated to make horseradish, whose flavor is that of radishes to the umpteenth power. Stirred into a paste with cider vinegar, finely grated horseradish adds a wonderful flavor to cole slaws and is an incomparable finish for boiled beef, poached chicken, fish, shellfish, gefilte fish, potatoes, beets, and seafood cocktail sauce. (Place about 1 pound diced peeled root in a food processor. Process until finely chopped, then pour in cider vinegar until the mixture is of a spreadable consistency. Add salt and a few tablespoons sugar to taste. This keeps several months in the refrigerator.) When the root is not in season (early spring), prepared horseradish sauce can be found in the grocery deli case. If using prepared horseradish, be sure to measure the amount the recipe calls for and drain the horseradish well before adding it to the rest of the ingredients.

Hot Apple Slaw

4 to 6 servings

This is a fine autumn salad. Granny Smith and other similarly tart apples work especially well here, though any cooking apple will do.

Cook in a large skillet over low heat until crisp:

6 slices thick-cut bacon

Drain the bacon on paper towels and crumble. Add to the fat in the skillet:

3 tablespoons cider vinegar
2 tablespoons water
1 tablespoon light or dark brown sugar
1 teaspoon caraway seeds, lightly crushed
Salt to taste

Bring to a boil, reduce the heat to a simmer, and stir in:

3 cups finely shredded red or green cabbage
1 large cooking apple, peeled, cored, and grated

Simmer for 2 minutes. Garnish with the crumbled bacon and serve hot.

Fennel and Mushroom Salad

6 to 8 servings

If you have a mandoline with which to slice the mushrooms and fennel, this salad comes together quickly (opposite).

Whisk together in a small bowl:

3 tablespoons extra-virgin olive oil
1 clove garlic, finely minced
½ to 1 tablespoon chopped fresh tarragon (optional)
Salt and ground black pepper to taste

Stir together in a medium bowl until the salt is dissolved:

¼ cup fresh lemon juice
Salt to taste

Add and toss to combine:

8 ounces mushrooms, wiped clean and thinly sliced
1 fennel bulb, thinly sliced

Pour the dressing over the vegetables and toss to coat evenly. Sprinkle with:

½ cup Parmesan cheese shavings

FENNEL

A bulb of fennel looks like a bunch of celery with a wide, round base. The individual stalks, which are beautifully plaited, are broad and thin, while the tops are round and fleshy. Fennel leaves are ferny, and the flavor of the whole plant is like licorice. (Some markets label it anise, which it is not.) Fennel is a rare cool-weather vegetable—it is harvested from midautumn through midspring. When shopping for fennel, select white bulbs with crisp, bright greens—no cuts, dark patches, or bruises. The rounder bulbs seem to be more tender than those that are really flat. Store in a perforated plastic bag in the refrigerator crisper. To prepare fennel, cut off the stalks and trim the base, discarding bruised or damaged outer layers. Fennel's feathery leaves make a nice garnish or can be chopped and used as an herb.

Celery Root Rémoulade

4 to 6 servings

More or less round in shape, celery root has a daunting appearance—knobby, grimy, and perhaps tangled at the roots. Ah, but beneath the skin is tender, cream-colored flesh with an exquisite nutty taste.

Wash well, peel, and cut into ¼-inch-thick rounds:

2 medium celery roots

Boil in salted water to cover for 3 to 4 minutes. Drain and let cool. Cut into very thin strips. Cover with:

Sauce Rémoulade, 119

allowing about ½ cup of sauce for every 2 cups celery root. Chill well and serve on a bed of:

Watercress, tough stems trimmed, washed and dried

Jícama Salad

8 servings

The lime and ground chili peppers in this recipe are the perfect complements to jícama's slightly sweet flavor. Its juicy, porous texture is reminiscent of an apple, though it is never mealy.

Peel and halve lengthwise:

1 medium jícama (about 1 pound)

Lay each half on its cut side, slice ¼ inch thick, and cut the slices diagonally in half. Cut diagonally into ¼-inch-thick slices:

2 small cucumbers, halved lengthwise and seeded

Cut a slice off the stem and blossom ends of:

3 medium navel oranges

Stand the oranges on a cutting board and cut away the peel and all the white pith. Halve lengthwise, then cut crosswise into ¼-inch-thick slices. In a large bowl, toss the jícama, cucumbers, and oranges along with:

6 radishes, thinly sliced
1 small red onion, thinly sliced
Juice of 2 limes (about ⅓ cup)

Let stand for 20 minutes, then season with:

Salt to taste

To serve, spoon the salad onto a platter and drizzle the accumulated juices on top. Sprinkle with:

About 2 teaspoons ground chili pepper, preferably ancho or guajillo
About ⅓ cup coarsely chopped fresh cilantro

Vegetable and Fruit Salad Cups

The bright, fresh, colorful nature of salads makes them feasts for the eyes as well as the palate. One of our favorite ways to present vegetable, grain, rice, bean, meat, poultry, and seafood salads is in hollowed-out cases made from vegetables and fruits.

On these pages, you'll find easy instructions for making five different types of vegetable and fruit serving cups. Page 58 offers details for an even more elaborate vessel, the Watermelon Basket. As widely varied as these are, they all rely on starting with fresh produce in the best possible condition. Make the extra effort to go to the best source you can find and then to select the best-formed, best-colored, most blemish-free specimens.

Although you can prepare these cups in advance, fill them as close to serving time as possible.

Cold Stuffed Tomatoes

Tomatoes can be cut and stuffed in a variety of ways to add a splash of color to any salad buffet. Almost any vegetable, grain, or combination salad goes well in tomatoes, but the best begin with ripe, good-tasting tomatoes. Whether or not to peel the tomatoes before stuffing is a personal choice. Keep in mind, however, that peeled tomatoes (particularly vine-ripened beauties) are especially delicate and best used to hold loosely packed vegetable salads such as

Cucumber Salad, 40, and cold *Celery Root Rémoulade*, 50. Other good choices for filling tomatoes are a rice salad, 72 to 75; *Couscous Salad*, 71; a cole slaw, 48–49; *Tabbouleh*, 69; *Seafood Salad*, 86; *Lobster Salad*, 88; *Egg Salad*, 102; *Chicken Salad*, 96; *Tuna Salad*, 102, and cottage cheese flavored with fresh herbs.

To prepare tomato cases, first peel the tomatoes if you wish. Slice off the round top of the tomato and, using a small serrated knife, cut around the inside to remove the core, pulp, and seeds, being careful to leave a thick-enough wall to support the case. The chopped tomato pulp can be mixed right into many salad recipes. You can also cut the tomatoes crosswise in half in a zigzag fashion and fill them, or fill hollowed-out halves separately. Before filling, salt the hollows lightly, invert the tomatoes, and let drain for 20 minutes. Chill and fill, allowing 1 stuffed tomato per person.

Avocado Salad Cups

Avocados have an unexpected affinity with shrimp, crab, and lobster, making them the perfect vehicle for serving these salads.

To prepare avocado cups, chill the avocados, then cut lengthwise in half. Remove the pit, shown 32. To prevent the fruit from darkening after cutting, sprinkle it with lemon juice. Mound the salad of your choice in the hollows left by the pits. Serve at room temperature.

Lettuce and Cabbage Cups

A bit more formal than serving a combination salad on a bed of greens, lettuce cups make an elegant display. The small, round, rather loosely bunched butterhead lettuces are ideal for salad cups. We also like the deep color of radicchio and red cabbage. Separate the leaves from the head carefully without tearing; wash and dry the leaves, sorting through to find enough evenly shaped ones for stuffing. Any imperfect leaves can go into the salad bowl. Just before serving, fill the leaves with any suitable salad you can think of, such as *Chicken Salad, 96, Lobster Salad, 88,* or any of the grain or bean salads, 64 to 71.

Cucumber Cups

Cucumber cups are refreshing on a luncheon plate or as an hors d'oeuvre, and their smaller size makes them more appropriate as a garnish than as a main course. Suitable fillings include *Chicken Salad, 96,* any seafood salad, 86 to 88, and any rice salad, 72 to 75, or other salad of small grains.

To prepare cucumber cups, first refrigerate small, shapely cucumbers until cold. Either peel the cucumbers or score the peel with a fork, shown 40. Waxed cucumbers should be peeled. Cut the cucumbers lengthwise in half, scoop out the seeds, and fill the halves. Alternatively, slice whole cucumbers crosswise into 2- to 3-inch pieces and hollow the pieces from one end, leaving enough on the bottom to prevent the filling from falling out.

Melon Cups

Ideal for a light luncheon, stuffed melon offers the cool refreshment of fruit combined with the savory substance of a meat or poultry salad.

To prepare melon cups, cut a cantaloupe or other melon in half. Remove the seeds and scallop the edges, if desired, for a more decorative effect. Refrigerate until cold. Just before serving, fill the melon with *Chicken Salad, 96, Turkey Salad with Chutney and Cashews, 98,* or a fruit salad.

ABOUT
FRUIT & MOLDED
SALADS

*F*resh fruit provides us with some of the simplest salads, well suited to serve for breakfast, brunch, or lunch, as part of a buffet, or for dessert. When fruits are cut up and combined, they often make their own dressing, too: a mingling of sweet juices that can be accented with fresh lemon or lime. Fruit salads also welcome embellishments, from nuts or sweet herbs; to the marshmallows and liqueur that sometimes enhance Ambrosia, 57; to the mayonnaise and diced celery that help define a classic Waldorf Salad, 57.

One delightful bonus of fruit salads is that a featured ingredient sometimes provides a serving vessel. Melon Cups, 53, are popular edible containers. A whole watermelon can make one of the most spectacular presentations of all, described in the recipe for Watermelon Fruit Basket, 58.

Fruits often star in a related salad category: molded salads, 61. Held in suspension by gelatin, their colorful shapes become almost jewellike, contributing to beautiful centerpieces for luncheon or dinner tables.

Waldorf Salad, 57

Fruit Salads

You can be sure a mix of fresh fruits will be pleasing when you base it on year-round favorites, then add bright colors and flavors from fruits of the season (good proportions are about 2 pounds foundation fruits and 1½ to 2 pounds seasonal fruits). To keep the mixture from looking like a hash, cut pieces in a variety of shapes, none smaller than bite-sized.

Fresh Fruit Salad

10 to 12 servings

Although it should be served to guests within a few hours, you can enjoy the salad for a day or two—citrus juices and honey keep the fruit from darkening. Add the following fruits and ingredients in the order given to a large mixing bowl, stirring gently every once in a while:

2 sweet oranges, peeled, seeded, and cut into bite-sized chunks
Juice of 1 large lemon
⅓ cup mild honey, preferably orange blossom, or sugar
2 green eating apples, cored and cut into medium dice
1 large banana, thinly sliced

1 large ripe pear, cored and cut into bite-sized chunks
Add 3 or 4 seasonal fruits, about 8 ounces each. Choose from:
Kiwis, peeled, cut lengthwise in half, and sliced
Strawberries, hulled and quartered lengthwise
Whole raspberries, blueberries, or blackberries
Pitted sweet cherries
Melon or watermelon balls
Peaches, nectarines, apricots, or plums, pitted and sliced
Seedless red grapes, stemmed

Summer Fruit Cup

2 servings

Halve and seed:
1 perfectly ripe small cantaloupe
Using the small end of a melon baller, make round balls of the cantaloupe by pressing the baller deep into the flesh until juice comes out of the hole in the bottom of the baller. Twist the melon baller to cut a whole ball and remove it to a bowl. Combine the melon balls with:
½ cup fresh sweet cherries, pitted
1 tablespoon orange juice

1 tablespoon crème de cassis or orange liqueur
Scoop out the remaining craters of flesh from the cantaloupe halves to make a smooth container (save the flesh for another use). Just before serving, gently toss the melon mixture with:
½ cup fresh raspberries, blackberries, or blueberries
Divide the fruit between the melon shells. Garnish with:
Fresh mint sprigs

Ambrosia

6 servings

Peel and section, right, into a bowl, adding all the juices:

6 navel oranges

Add and gently combine:

3 bananas, sliced

½ cup miniature marshmallows (optional)

½ pineapple, cut into ½-inch cubes

½ cup shredded sweetened dried coconut

3 tablespoons orange liqueur (optional)

Cover and refrigerate until ready to serve.

PEELING AND SECTIONING CITRUS FRUITS

Segmenting the fruit for a salad or dessert takes a little time—and is worth it. Slice off the top and bottom of the round fruit, down to the flesh. Stand the fruit on a cutting board and use a serrated knife to cut off the rind in even slices. Trim away any remaining white membrane. Free each segment by cutting down against the membrane on either side. Lift out the segment and remove any seeds. Squeeze all the juice from the membranes into a bowl. The best way to slice citrus very thin is to have the fruit chilled and use a thin, sharp knife.

Winter Fruit Salad

3 or 4 servings

Peel and section, right, into a bowl, adding all the juices:

1 grapefruit

1 orange

Refrigerate until cold. Not long before serving, add:

1 apple, quartered, cored, and thinly sliced

1 banana, sliced

Stir to coat the flesh with citrus juice to prevent discoloration. Stir in:

1 small bunch seedless red grapes, stemmed and halved

Spoon the fruit salad into serving bowls.

Texas-Style Watermelon Salad

4 to 6 servings

We knew an old-time Texan who liked his watermelon dusted with salt and pepper; this recipe takes that strange-sounding but delicious notion a little further with the addition of chili peppers.

Stir together in a small bowl:

½ teaspoon chili powder

½ teaspoon salt, or to taste

⅛ teaspoon ground red pepper, or to taste

Toss together in a serving bowl:

2 pounds watermelon, seeds and rind discarded, flesh cut into ½-inch pieces (about 4 cups)

½ red onion, diced

1 small jalapeño pepper, seeded and diced

3 tablespoons fresh lime juice, or to taste

2 tablespoons minced fresh cilantro or fresh parsley

Sprinkle with the spice mixture and toss well. Serve immediately.

Waldorf Salad

4 to 6 servings

Created by Chef Oscar Tschirky of the Waldorf-Astoria Hotel in New York in the late 1890s, this salad was considered the height of sophistication in the early years of this century. Originally it contained nothing more than apples, celery, and mayonnaise. Chopped wal-nuts and seeded grape halves came later. A version popular with children (and some adults) includes miniature marshmallows.

Combine in a medium bowl:

1 cup diced celery

1 cup diced firm apples

½ cup coarsely chopped walnuts (optional)

½ cup seedless red grapes, halved (optional)

Stir in:

½ to ¾ cup mayonnaise

Serve at room temperature or cold.

Watermelon Fruit Basket

About 14 servings

This is always a thrill to serve. Everything can be prepared 3 to 4 hours in advance for combining at serving time. An icebox watermelon can be prepared the same way, using a proportionately smaller amount of fruit.
Rinse and wipe dry:

**1 ripe 12- to 14-pound
watermelon**

With a long, sharp serrated knife, cut a thin, flat slice off one long side of the melon (**1**) to keep it from wobbling. Slice the melon lengthwise in two (**2**), cutting about 1 inch above the center. Lift off the top. Remove the flesh in the heart of the melon with a melon baller (**3**), or use a teaspoon to scoop out egg shapes. Cover and refrigerate 4 cups watermelon balls. Scoop out the rest of the flesh (save it for another purpose), leaving about ½ inch of red flesh lining the shell. Stand the shell upside down in a cool place to drain. Pour into a large mixing bowl:

2 cups fresh orange juice
You will need about 10 cups fruit in addition to the watermelon to fill the basket. For the most refreshing mix, use unpeeled summer fruits and berries, cut up no smaller than bite-sized. With the watermelon balls, we like richly colored, firm ripe fruits such as:

Whole small strawberries, hulled
Blackberries
Blueberries
**Cantaloupe or honeydew melon
balls**
Sliced nectarines
Sliced plums of any color
**Sliced kiwis or seedless green
grapes**

Cut up the fruits and toss with the orange juice to keep them from darkening. Cover and refrigerate. Sugar should not be necessary. Just before serving, add the watermelon to the other fruit along with:

3 tablespoons chopped fresh mint
Toss gently together with your hands and fill the melon shell (save the juices in the bowl to drink). If desired, top with:

**14 scoops (about 3 pints)
best-quality sorbet or sherbet**
Serve at once, ladling into dessert bowls.

WATERMELONS

Indicative of their name, watermelons are composed of 90–95 percent water. This favorite summertime fruit falls into four main groups: icebox, Crimson sweet, jubilee, and allsweet. Within these categories, characteristics such as fruit shape, rind pattern, flesh color, and presence or absence of seeds vary, but all are wonderfully low in calories and contain no cholesterol. Although traditionally watermelon flesh is red, there is no major difference in taste whether the flesh is red or yellow.

Golden Glow Gelatin Salad

8 servings

The pineapple and carrots virtually vibrate with color (opposite).
Drain, reserving the juice:

One 20-ounce can crushed pineapple

Add enough water to the reserved juice to make 2 cups total and bring to a boil in a small saucepan. Place in a medium bowl:

One 3-ounce package orange-flavored gelatin
One 3-ounce package pineapple-flavored gelatin

Add the hot liquid and stir until the gelatin is dissolved. Stir in:

2 cups cold water

Refrigerate until the gelatin is as thick as raw egg whites, 1 to 1½ hours. Fold in the reserved pineapple along with:

4 cups grated carrots

Rinse an 8-cup mold or bowl, then shake out the excess water. Pour in the gelatin mixture, cover, and refrigerate until set, about 3 hours. Unmold, below, or serve from the bowl.

Creamy Cucumber Gelatin Salad

6 to 8 servings

This is one of the most sophisticated gelatin molds we have come across and makes a stunning first course.
Combine in a medium bowl and let stand for 10 minutes:

1 medium cucumber, peeled, seeded, and diced
4 cups water
2 teaspoons salt

Drain the cucumbers, then toss with:

1 tablespoon lemon juice

Let stand in a small bowl for 5 minutes to soften:

2¼ teaspoons (1 envelope) unflavored gelatin
2 tablespoons cold water

Add and stir until the gelatin is dissolved:

¼ cup scalded milk

Add the gelatin mixture to the cucumbers along with:

1 teaspoon white wine tarragon vinegar
½ teaspoon salt

Whip until stiff peaks form and fold into the cucumbers in 2 additions:

1 cup heavy cream

Rinse a 4-cup ring mold or bowl, then shake out the excess water. Spoon in the cucumber mixture and smooth the top. Refrigerate for 12 hours.

Combine in a medium bowl 1 hour before serving:

1 pound cooked medium shrimp, peeled and deveined
3 tablespoons minced fresh parsley
½ cup *Basic Vinaigrette*, 108

Unmold, below, top with the cooked shrimp, and serve.

Apple-Currant Gelatin Salad

4 to 6 servings

Apple juice and ginger ale give this salad a wonderful fall flavor.
Whisk together in a medium bowl until the gelatin is dissolved:

One 3-ounce package orange-flavored gelatin
1 cup boiling apple juice

Stir in:

1 cup ginger ale

Refrigerate until the gelatin is as thick as raw egg whites, 1 to 1½ hours. Fold in:

⅔ cup grated peeled apples
¼ cup currants

Rinse a 3- to 4-cup bowl or mold with cold water, then shake the excess water out. Pour in the gelatin mixture and refrigerate until set, about 3 hours. Unmold, right, or serve from the bowl.

UNMOLDING GELATIN

Dip the mold into a sink filled with very hot tap water. Metal molds should be dipped for no longer than a couple of seconds, but thick molds of glass or ceramic may need to be warmed for as long as 10 seconds before they will release. Invert the gelatin onto a plate.

ABOUT
BEAN &
GRAIN
SALADS

*T*he mild flavors and chewy textures of beans, rice, pasta, and other grains are a perfect backdrop for a variety of salads. Fresh vegetables, seasonings, meat, and poultry are added for contrast and flavor, making these versatile side dishes or healthy meals unto themselves. These salads take a bit of advance preparation, since the beans, rice, pasta, and grains must first be cooked, but once made, they hold up well. If the salad has been refrigerated, let it stand at room temperature for a bit before serving, taste and adjust the seasonings (starches tend to absorb seasonings over time), and serve at room temperature.

The salads that follow are best made from beans, rice, pasta, and grains that are cooked to firm-tender. Boost the flavor of rice, grains, and beans by cooking in stock or broth with a few aromatic vegetables. Pastas should be cooked until tender but firm. Canned beans can easily be substituted for dried. Whatever the base, be sure everything is well drained, lest it dilute the dressing, and, as with potatoes, toss these salads while still warm to absorb the most flavor from the dressing.

White Bean Salad with Green Olives, 66

Black Bean Salad

4 to 6 servings

This Southwestern salad is better the day after it's made.

Combine in a large bowl and mix well:

4 cups cooked black beans (about 1⅓ cups dried), opposite, rinsed and drained if canned

½ red onion, diced
½ red bell pepper, diced
½ cup fresh lime juice
3 tablespoons coarsely chopped fresh cilantro or fresh parsley
1 scallion, white part only, minced
1 tablespoon ground cumin

Generous dash of ground red pepper
Salt and ground black pepper to taste

Serve at room temperature or slightly chilled.

Chickpea Salad

4 servings

Chickpeas are rich in vitamins A and C, high in fiber, and a good source of calcium and iron.

Combine in a medium bowl:

2 cups canned chickpeas, rinsed and drained
½ small red onion, minced

3 tablespoons minced fresh parsley
2½ tablespoons fresh lemon juice
2 tablespoons extra-virgin olive oil
1 teaspoon Dijon mustard
1 to 2 cloves garlic, minced
Salt and ground black pepper to taste

On a platter, make a bed of:

4 cups shredded chicory, escarole, or romaine lettuce, washed and dried

Spoon the chickpea salad on top and serve at room temperature.

HOW TO SOAK BEANS

1 Spread legumes in a pan or large colander and remove any tiny stones that may have accompanied them out of the field.

2 Rinse the beans very well under cold water, raking them with your fingers. This will get rid of any remaining clumps of dirt.

3 Our preferred soaking method is to heat the soaking water, which hastens the swelling of the beans. For a gentle quick-soak, pour boiling water over the beans to cover by 2 inches. Cover, let stand until the beans have swelled to at least twice their size and have absorbed most of the water, and then drain. This will take at least an hour, but the beans will remain firm and keep their shape when cooked.

HOW TO COOK BEANS

1 To cook beans, place them in a large pot and add cold water to cover by 2 inches.

2 Bring to a boil over high heat; skim off the foam that rises to the surface.

3 Reduce the heat to low and cover; simmer, stirring and skimming occasionally, until the beans are tender. Do not boil rapidly or the abrasion will loosen the bean skins. If the pot threatens to boil over, partially remove the cover. Cook beans uncovered if you have seasoned the liquid and want some of it to evaporate to concentrate the flavor or to thicken the dish. You can simmer beans with chopped onions and carrots to sweeten them. For relatively firm beans, remove a few beans and pinch them for tenderness at the low end of the cooking time range. If soaked first, most beans will cook in 1 to 1½ hours. The exceptions are small beans, such as lentils and flageolets, which generally cook in 20 to 30 minutes even without presoaking.

Warm Black-Eyed Pea Salad

4 servings

This salad is "warm" in two ways. Earthy black-eyed peas are a good foil for other earthy flavors, such as sage, and also for heat. We recommend that you use at least 10 dashes of the hot red pepper sauce of your choice in this recipe.

Heat in a medium nonstick saucepan or skillet over medium heat:

¼ cup chicken stock
1½ tablespoons olive oil

Add:

1 large sweet red onion, diced
2 cloves garlic, minced

Cook, stirring occasionally, until the onion is softened, 4 to 5 minutes.

Add:

4 cups cooked black-eyed peas (about 1⅓ cups dried), above
1 tablespoon minced fresh sage
Salt to taste
10 dashes hot red pepper sauce, or to taste

Cook, stirring occasionally, about 3 minutes. Remove from the heat and stir in:

2 tablespoons sherry or red wine vinegar, or to taste

Serve warm or at room temperature, garnished with:

Small sprigs fresh sage

Georgian Kidney Bean Salad

6 to 8 appetizer servings

The cooking of Georgia is the spiciest—and many say the best—in all of the former Soviet Union. It is said that Georgians measure a stranger by the gusto (and capacity) with which he or she eats. You can replace the cooked beans with one 19-ounce can kidney beans, rinsed and drained.

Pick over, rinse, and soak, 64:

8 ounces dried red kidney beans

Drain and place the beans in a saucepan. Add water to cover by 2 inches along with:

1 small onion, peeled and halved

1 clove garlic, peeled but left whole

1 bay leaf

Bring to a boil over high heat, reduce the heat to low, and simmer, covered, until the beans are tender but not mushy, about 1 hour. Drain and discard the onion, garlic, and bay leaf. Remove the beans to a medium bowl. Stir in:

⅓ cup plum jam

2 tablespoons red wine vinegar

1 to 2 tablespoons minced fresh cilantro

1 tablespoon fresh lemon juice

½ small fresh jalapeño or other small chili pepper, seeded and minced

1 clove garlic, minced

½ teaspoon salt

¼ teaspoon ground coriander

Ground black pepper to taste

Taste and adjust the seasonings and serve at room temperature.

White Bean Salad with Green Olives

4 to 6 servings

Add a drained can of tuna to this salad and you can transform it into a lunch or dinner entrée.

Combine in a medium bowl:

3 cups cooked white kidney beans (about 1 cup dried), 65, or other white beans, rinsed and drained if canned

2 small celery stalks, thinly sliced

15 Spanish olives, pitted and sliced

2 tablespoons chopped fresh tarragon or parsley

Whisk together:

1 tablespoon red wine vinegar

1 clove garlic, minced

½ teaspoon sweet paprika

¼ teaspoon salt

Whisk in:

3 to 4 tablespoons olive oil, preferably extra virgin

Pour the dressing over the bean mixture and toss gently to coat. Season with:

Ground black pepper to taste

Serve at room temperature.

Lentil and Red Potato Salad with Warm Sherry Vinaigrette

4 servings

Make this close to serving time so that it can be consumed while still warm. It goes well with grilled sausages and braised escarole or other greens.

Cook in boiling water until tender, about 15 minutes:

12 ounces small red potatoes, halved if larger than 1 inch in diameter

Drain and cut into small cubes when cool enough to handle. Combine in a large bowl:

½ cup thinly sliced scallions

½ cup chopped fresh parsley

Add the potato cubes along with:

4½ cups warm cooked green or brown lentils (about 1½ cups dried), 65

Whisk together in a small saucepan:

¼ cup extra-virgin olive oil

3 tablespoons sherry vinegar

1 clove garlic, very finely minced

½ teaspoon salt

⅛ teaspoon ground black pepper

Heat, stirring, until warm. Pour over the lentil mixture and serve.

Three-Bean Salad

4 to 6 servings

This American salad-bar classic actually tastes better the next day.

Boil in salted water to cover until tender but still slightly crunchy, about 2 minutes:

1 cup ½-inch pieces green beans

1 cup ½-inch pieces yellow wax beans

Drain and place in a large bowl. Add and stir to combine:

One 16-ounce can kidney beans, rinsed and drained

½ cup chopped green bell pepper

½ cup chopped onion

Whisk together in a small bowl or shake in a small covered jar:

½ cup vegetable oil

½ cup tarragon vinegar or red wine vinegar

¾ cup sugar

1 teaspoon minced fresh tarragon, or ½ teaspoon dried

1 teaspoon salt

½ teaspoon ground black pepper

Pour the dressing over the bean mixture and toss well to coat. Cover and refrigerate for at least 6 hours or overnight. Serve cold. If desired, serve in:

Lettuce cups, 53

CANNED BEANS

Canned beans can be substituted cup for cup in recipes that call for cooked beans, but they are almost always softer and less flavorful. Since brands vary in quality, it is worth trying different ones. Rinsing canned beans improves the taste and removes excess salt. To rinse, put the beans in a large sieve set in a bowl and let cold water run over them until the bowl is filled, raking the beans with your fingers; drain, repeat, and then drain well.

Tabbouleh

4 to 6 servings

Tabbouleh (opposite) is a popular Middle Eastern salad and makes a particularly refreshing summer dish. The following recipe is fairly standard, but there are many variations using chopped cucumbers, red onions, dill, and basil, even crumbled feta cheese. Traditionally tabbouleh is scooped up and eaten with leaves of romaine lettuce.

Combine in a large bowl:

1 cup medium bulgur
2 cups boiling water

Cover with an inverted plate and let stand for 30 minutes. Drain in a sieve, pressing with the back of a large spoon to remove the excess moisture, and return to the bowl. Add:

4 large ripe tomatoes, finely chopped
2 cups fresh parsley sprigs, finely chopped
1 cup packed fresh mint sprigs, finely chopped
1 cup packed purslane, washed, dried, and finely chopped (optional)
1 bunch scallions, finely chopped
1 medium onion, finely chopped

Stir in:

½ teaspoon ground allspice (optional)
½ teaspoon salt
¼ teaspoon ground black pepper

Whisk together:

⅓ cup fresh lemon juice
⅓ cup olive oil

Add to the bulgur and toss to coat. Spoon the salad onto a platter and surround with:

1 head romaine lettuce, separated into leaves, washed, and dried

Serve at room temperature.

BULGUR

Bulgur is available in fine, medium, and coarse grinds. Because it is steamed before it is dried and cracked, it can be softened and made ready to eat by soaking in boiling water without cooking. This method is often used for salads.

Barley, Mushroom, and Asparagus Salad

4 to 6 servings

Cook in a large pot of boiling salted water until tender, about 40 minutes:

1 cup pearl barley

While the barley is cooking, heat in a small skillet over medium heat:

3 tablespoons olive oil

Add:

2 shallots, minced

Cook, stirring, until softened, about 2 minutes. Add:

1 cup sliced fresh morel or other wild and/or cultivated mushrooms

Cook, stirring, until the mushrooms have released their liquid and are softened and the liquid is evaporated, about 3 minutes. Stir in:

1 tablespoon fresh lemon juice
1 tablespoon minced fresh parsley
½ teaspoon finely grated lemon zest
Salt and ground black pepper to taste

Remove from the heat. When the barley is tender, add to the pot and cook until bright green and crisp-tender, about 4 minutes:

6 ounces pencil-thin asparagus, cut diagonally into 1-inch pieces

Drain the barley and asparagus thoroughly in a colander. Combine the mushroom and barley mixtures; taste and adjust the seasonings. Serve warm.

Quinoa Salad with Pine Nuts and Raisins

4 servings

Both couscous and fine bulgur can be substituted for the quinoa in this recipe. (To do so, cook the couscous according to directions for Couscous Salad, opposite, or soak fine bulgur, 69.) You can also mix couscous and bulgur together for an interesting variation.

Rinse in a fine-mesh sieve and drain:

1 cup quinoa

Heat in a large, deep skillet over medium heat:

1 tablespoon olive oil

Add and cook, stirring constantly to avoid burning the garlic:

1 clove garlic, finely minced

Add the quinoa and cook, stirring constantly, until the grains are separate and golden. Stir in:

2 cups water
½ teaspoon salt

Bring to a boil, reduce the heat, and simmer until the liquid is absorbed, 12 to 15 minutes. Fluff with a fork and let cool.

Add and toss to coat:

¼ cup *Lime Vinaigrette*, 108, prepared with cumin seeds

Add and toss to combine:

¼ cup pine nuts, toasted (below)
1 yellow bell pepper, very finely diced
6 dried apricots, finely chopped
3 tablespoons golden raisins
2 tablespoons dried currants
2 tablespoons chopped fresh cilantro or snipped fresh chives

Season with:

Salt to taste

Add more dressing if desired.

QUINOA

The name, pronounced "keenwa," puzzles at first, and its botanical origins are not truly those of a grain but of a weed related to lamb's quarters. Yet quinoa, cultivated in the Andes by Inca farmers hundreds of years ago, is an eminently practical grain for everyday eating, for it cooks fast and is high in protein and minerals. The taste and texture tease with lightness and a very faint herbal quality. Quinoa becomes rancid quickly, so refrigerate it.

TOASTING NUTS

Toasting nuts crisps them and brings out their flavor. To toast nuts in the oven, spread them blanched or unblanched on an ungreased baking sheet and bake in a 325°F oven for 5 to 7 minutes, checking and stirring often to prevent burning. To toast nuts on top of the stove, place them in a dry skillet over medium heat and cook, stirring or shaking the pan frequently to prevent burning, until they just begin to release their fragrance, about 4 minutes. Let toasted nuts cool completely. Toasted nuts can be stored, covered, in a cool, dry place for up to 2 weeks.

Couscous Salad

4 to 6 servings

Combine in a large bowl:

1 box (about 1¾ cups) quick-cooking couscous

2¼ cups boiling water

Cover and let stand until the water is absorbed and the couscous has expanded, about 15 minutes. Fluff with a fork. As soon as the couscous is cool enough to handle, rub your hands with olive oil and gently rub the couscous between your fingertips to make sure all the lumps are out. Stir in:

½ cup diced peeled carrots

½ cup diced celery

1 tablespoon grated lemon or lime zest

2 tablespoons chopped fresh mint

2 tablespoons chopped fresh parsley

2 teaspoons ground cumin

Salt and ground black pepper to taste

Whisk together until smooth:

¼ cup olive oil

3 tablespoons lemon juice

1 teaspoon ground turmeric

Add to the salad, stir well to moisten, and serve warm or chilled.

Rice Salad with Chicken and Black Olives

4 servings

This recipe can be used as a blueprint for many kinds of rice salads. Simmer the rice in chicken stock for more flavor. As a general rule, use 3 cups cooked rice for roughly an equal amount of other ingredients (vegetables, fruit, chicken, seafood, etc.), cooked, if necessary, and chopped into bite-sized pieces. Toss with about ½ cup dressing of your choice.

Bring to a boil in a medium saucepan:

2½ to 3 cups water

1½ tablespoons butter or vegetable oil (optional)

½ to ¾ teaspoon salt

Add and stir once:

1½ cups long-grain white rice

Cover and cook over low heat until all the water is absorbed, 15 to 18 minutes. Do not lift the cover before the end of cooking. Let stand, covered, for 5 to 10 minutes. Stir together in a medium bowl:

1½ cups diced cooked chicken

½ cup diced peaches (about 1 medium)

½ cup coarsely chopped pitted oil-cured black olives

½ cup diced red or yellow bell peppers

Add the rice while still warm along with:

½ cup *Fresh Herb Vinaigrette*, 108

Toss well to combine. Serve warm, at room temperature, or chilled.

RICE SALAD WITH CHICKEN AND PISTACHIOS

Prepare the rice for Rice Salad with Chicken and Black Olives, above. Toss with 3 cups diced cooked chicken; ¾ cup shelled unsalted pistachios; 1 medium red onion, finely diced; ½ cup chopped flat-leaf parsley; 6 fresh basil leaves, chopped; ¼ cup drained capers; ⅓ cup olive oil; the grated zest and juice of 1 lemon; and salt and ground black pepper to taste. Serve at room temperature.

Rice Salad with Sun-Dried Tomatoes

4 servings

Prepare the rice for *Rice Salad with Chicken and Black Olives, above.*
Whisk together:

6 oil-packed sun-dried tomato halves, minced

6 tablespoons olive oil

3 tablespoons balsamic vinegar

1 clove garlic, minced

1 teaspoon chili powder

¼ teaspoon ground cumin

¼ teaspoon ground coriander

Stir into the warm rice along with:

4 more sun-dried tomato halves, diced

¼ cup pine nuts, toasted

4 scallions, minced

Salt and ground black pepper to taste

Serve warm or at room temperature (opposite).

Wild Rice Salad with Sausage

4 to 6 servings

The nutty taste of wild rice balances the sweet grapes and savory sausage. For a lunch or supper entrée, serve this salad on a bed of lightly dressed Boston lettuce or curly-leaf red or green lettuce leaves.

Whisk together in a small bowl:

2 tablespoons champagne vinegar or white wine vinegar

1 tablespoon Dijon mustard

Whisk in:

⅓ cup olive oil

Salt and ground black pepper to taste

Cook, stirring, in a medium skillet over medium heat until cooked through, breaking the meat up with the side of a spoon:

1 pound sweet Italian sausage, casings removed

Drain on paper towels, pat dry, let cool, and remove to a large bowl. Combine with:

2¼ cups Basic Cooked Wild Rice, opposite, (about ¾ cup uncooked), rinsed and drained

2¼ cups cooked long-grain white rice (about ¾ cup uncooked), rinsed and drained

3 inner celery stalks with leaves, thinly sliced

12 ounces seedless green or red grapes, halved (optional)

Add the dressing and toss well to coat. Taste and adjust the seasonings. Serve at room temperature.

Basic Cooked Wild Rice

3½ cups; 4 to 6 servings

Wild rice is done when most of the kernels are cracked, revealing the fluffy white interior. If the water evaporates before the rice is done, simply add more water, about ¼ cup at a time.

Combine in a large saucepan:

3 cups water

1 cup wild rice, rinsed and drained

1 teaspoon salt (optional)

Bring to a boil. Stir once, cover, and simmer over low heat until the water is absorbed and the rice is fluffy and tender, 35 to 55 minutes. Let stand, covered, for 10 minutes before serving.

Brown Rice Salad with Dates and Oranges

4 servings

This salad takes its flavor inspiration from North Africa.

Bring to a boil in a medium saucepan:

2 to 2½ cups water

1 tablespoon butter (optional)

¼ to ½ teaspoon salt

Add and stir once:

1 cup brown rice

Cover and cook over very low heat until all the water is absorbed, 35 to 45 minutes. Do not lift the cover before the end of cooking. Let stand, covered, for 5 to 10 minutes. Transfer the rice to a large bowl. Add and toss to combine:

16 dates, pitted and diced

2 large navel oranges, peeled, divided into segments, 57, each segment cut into thirds

2 scallions, minced

¼ cup dark or golden raisins

¼ cup minced fresh parsley

¼ cup extra-virgin olive oil

2 tablespoons fresh lemon juice

¼ teaspoon ground cinnamon

¼ teaspoon ground cumin

Pinch of red pepper flakes

Salt to taste

Serve at room temperature.

Brown Rice and Tofu Salad with Orange Sesame Dressing

6 servings

Smoked tofu is also an excellent choice for this salad. Black beans or any other preferred beans can be substituted for the adzukis. Basmati, which in Sanskrit means "Queen of Fragrance," has an alluring nutlike aroma and flavor. Between the flavor of basmati and the freshness of the orange dressing, this hearty salad is an irresistible dish.

Shake together in a tightly covered jar:

½ cup canola oil
4 teaspoons toasted sesame oil
⅓ cup orange juice
⅓ cup seasoned rice vinegar
1 small fresh jalapeño pepper, seeded and minced
1 teaspoon minced peeled fresh ginger
1 teaspoon minced garlic

Chill. Combine in a large bowl:

4 cups warm cooked brown basmati rice (about 1½ cups uncooked)
One 10½-ounce package extra-firm tofu, cut into ¾-inch cubes
3 cups cooked adzuki beans (about 1 cup dried), 65, rinsed and drained if canned
½ cup chopped red onions
1 cup chopped bell peppers, preferably half red and half green
¼ cup finely chopped fresh cilantro

Shake the dressing well, pour over the rice mixture, and toss well to coat. Season with:

Salt and ground black pepper to taste

Line a serving platter with:

Lettuce leaves

Spoon the salad on the leaves and sprinkle with:

1 tablespoon sesame seeds, toasted

Serve immediately.

ADZUKI BEANS

Also called aduki or azuki beans, these small, claret red, mild-tasting beans add color contrast to grain salads and can be substituted for small red beans, although they are more fragile in texture and much lighter in taste. They are also used to make the red bean paste used in Chinese buns and other sweets. The flavor of adzuki beans is faintly reminiscent of black-eyed peas. Both adzukis and black-eyed peas are in the mung bean family. Soak the beans, 64, in water to cover. Drain and place in a pan with water to cover by 2 inches. Simmer, covered, until tender, 30 to 40 minutes. It is important to begin testing the beans for tenderness at the low end of the cooking time.

Pasta Salad

4 to 6 servings

Try substituting fresh or reconstituted dried chili peppers for the red pepper flakes in this pasta salad (opposite). Try different fresh herbs, or add diced cheese or diced cooked meat, such as ham, chicken, or lamb. For a creamy pasta salad, substitute ½ cup mayonnaise for the oil, vinegar, and chicken stock. Recipes for homemade mayonnaise begin on page 116.

Combine in a large bowl while the pasta is still warm:

8 ounces elbow macaroni, penne, wagon wheel, or other pasta, cooked until tender but firm, rinsed with cool water, and drained
3 tablespoons extra-virgin olive oil
3 tablespoons white wine vinegar
2 tablespoons chicken stock
Salt and ground black pepper to taste

Let cool to room temperature.
Stir in:

12 cherry tomatoes, halved
12 yellow plum tomatoes, quartered
½ cup finely diced red onion
12 oil-cured black olives, pitted and coarsely chopped
¼ cup minced fresh basil
¼ cup minced fresh parsley
2 tablespoons minced fresh mint
1 teaspoon finely grated lemon zest

Taste and adjust the seasonings.
Serve at room temperature.

Pasta Salad Primavera with Pesto

4 to 8 servings

This is an easy spring dish that lends itself to improvisation. Any seasonal vegetable can be substituted.

Place in a large pot of boiling salted water and cook for 2 minutes:

1 large bunch broccoli, cut into small flowers (about 1½ cups)
2 medium carrots, peeled and finely diced
¾ cup fresh or frozen peas

Remove the vegetables with a large strainer and cool under cold running water. Return the water to a boil. Add and cook until tender but firm:

1 pound penne

Drain and rinse under cold running water. In a large serving bowl, combine the pasta and cooked vegetables along with:

1 red or yellow bell pepper, finely diced
1 medium red onion, finely diced

Toss with:

1 recipe *Pesto Sauce, below*

Serve at room temperature. This salad can be made ahead and refrigerated, but it is best to bring it back to room temperature before serving.

Pesto Sauce

Enough for 1 pound pasta

This classic sauce from Genoa needs to be made with fresh basil.

Process to a rough paste in a food processor:

2 cups loosely packed fresh basil leaves
⅓ cup pine nuts
2 medium cloves garlic, peeled
½ cup grated Parmesan cheese

With the machine running, slowly pour through the feed tube:

½ cup extra-virgin olive oil

If the sauce seems dry (it should be a thick paste), add a little more olive oil.
Season with:

Salt and ground black pepper to taste

Use immediately or store in a covered glass jar in the refrigerator for up to 1 week.

Pasta Salad with Avocado and Grilled Chicken

4 to 6 servings

A thoroughly American treatment for pasta using favorite foods—avocado and grilled chicken. The dish can also be made with leftover baked or broiled chicken.

Combine well in a large bowl:

3 boneless, skinless chicken breast halves (about 1 pound), grilled and cut into thin strips

1 large ripe Hass avocado, peeled and finely diced

1 pound fusilli, cooked until tender but firm, rinsed with cool water, and drained

3 medium, ripe tomatoes, seeded and chopped

4 scallions, thinly sliced

2 cloves garlic, finely minced

¼ cup drained capers

¼ cup chopped fresh basil, cilantro, or parsley

¼ cup olive oil, or more to taste

Juice of 1 lemon

Salt and ground black pepper to taste

Serve at room temperature. It is best to serve this salad soon after it is made because the avocado tends to darken. If you need to make it ahead, dice and add the avocado just before serving.

Pasta Salad with Shrimp, Roasted Red Peppers, and Black Olives

4 to 6 servings

Because shrimp is so good cold, it is a natural for a light pasta salad. For more flavor in the salad, boil the shrimp in the shell first and then use the same water to cook the pasta. This salad refrigerates well, but bring it closer to room temperature before serving.

Roast, opposite:

4 red bell peppers

Peel, seed, and cut into thin strips.

Toss together in a large bowl:

1 pound penne, fusilli, or other pasta, cooked until tender but firm, rinsed with cool water, and drained

⅓ cup olive oil

1 clove garlic, minced

Add the roasted peppers along with:

1 pound medium shrimp, boiled, shelled, and deveined

½ cup pitted oil-cured black olives

½ cup chopped fresh flat-leaf parsley

¼ cup pine nuts, toasted

Pinch of ground red pepper

Salt and ground black pepper to taste

Toss well to coat and combine. Serve at room temperature.

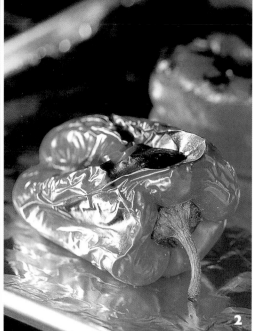
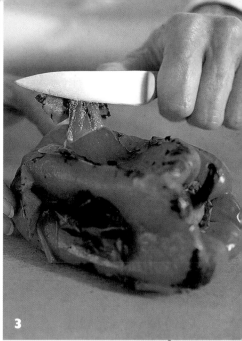

HOW TO ROAST AND PEEL PEPPERS

Roasting provides the best way to remove the skin of peppers. It softens their flesh, tempers the raw taste, and adds a delicious smokiness. Thick-walled peppers can be taken a step further and charred. Thinner-walled peppers are better if blistered but not completely charred, or they will lose flesh when you peel them. Red peppers tend to char faster than green ones, having more sugars in their flesh.

1 *Stove-Roasting Fresh Peppers:* If you have a gas cooktop, this is the simplest method. If not, use the broiler method. Place whole peppers directly in the flames of your gas burner on its highest setting. Keep an eye on the peppers and turn them frequently with metal tongs, letting the peppers blister or char (do not pierce with a cooking fork, as juices will be lost). Continue roasting the peppers until the entire surface is blistered. Many cooks quickly toast, or stove-roast, dried chili peppers before rehydrating them, to deepen and round out flavors.

2 *Broiler-Roasting Fresh Peppers:* Line a broiler pan with aluminum foil. Place whole peppers on the foil and brush with olive oil. Broil, turning as needed, until blackened on all sides. Brush the skin with oil. Place the pepper skin side up on a broiling pan and set the pan 5 to 6 inches under the broiler. Broil until the skin starts to blister and brown in places, watching it at every moment. Let the pieces char if you wish the flesh to be well cooked.

Grill-Roasting Fresh Peppers: This is the most flavorful method. Set whole peppers on a rack over ash-covered coals, a hot but dying fire. Let them sit in one place until they are blistered or charred, turn and repeat until the whole pepper is done.

Griddle- or Skillet-Roasting Fresh Peppers: This is for small fresh chilies such as serranos and jalapeños. Heat a dry cast-iron griddle or skillet over high heat, add the whole peppers, and shake them around the skillet until their skins are charred here and there. These chilies are customarily not peeled after roasting, but they may be.

3 *Peeling Roasted Peppers:* Once they are blistered, lay the peppers in a bowl and cover with a plate or plastic wrap. Let stand for at least 10 minutes, preferably 20 minutes or more. Their heat will create steam, which will loosen the skins. Try not to rinse peppers after roasting, for much of the smoky flavor is on the surface. Scrape off the skins with a knife. If the peppers were whole, make a slit down one side, then run the tip of a small knife around the stem underneath the base. Remove the top and the core and seeds, then scrape away remaining seeds and cut away the membranes. Add any juices in the bottom of the bowl to the dish you are making, or blend them into a vinaigrette dressing for added flavor. Roasting and peeling can be done a day or two in advance. If you do so, wrap the peppers airtight and store in the refrigerator.

Penne Salad with Feta and Olives

4 to 6 servings

Since both feta and capers are salty, taste this salad before adding any salt.
Mince together:
½ cup fresh parsley leaves
2 tablespoons drained capers (optional)
1 tablespoon fresh oregano leaves
1 small fresh jalapeño or other chili pepper, seeded if less heat is desired
2 cloves garlic
Place in a serving bowl along with:
⅓ cup extra-virgin olive oil
Stir in:
5 to 6 ounces feta cheese, coarsely crumbled
About 12 Kalamata olives, pitted and finely chopped
Salt if needed and ground black pepper to taste
Cook in a large pot of boiling salted water until tender but firm:
1 pound penne
Place in a colander:
½ small red onion, cut into rings
Drain the pasta onto the onion in the colander and immediately add both to the feta mixture. Toss gently to coat and combine. Serve at room temperature.

Creamy Macaroni Salad (Reduced Fat)

4 servings

This salad has less than 140 calories per serving.
Set a very fine mesh sieve or a colander lined with a coffee filter or several layers of cheesecloth over a bowl. Add and let drain at room temperature for at least 2 hours or covered in the refrigerator for up to 24 hours:
½ cup plus 2 tablespoons nonfat yogurt
Transfer the yogurt to a bowl. Add and whisk together:
1 clove garlic, minced
1½ teaspoons red wine vinegar
1 teaspoon sugar
Salt and ground black pepper to taste
Add and toss to coat:
4 ounces elbow macaroni, cooked until tender but firm, rinsed with cool water, and drained
Stir in:
½ cup finely chopped red, yellow, or orange bell peppers, or a combination
½ cup very thinly sliced fennel
3 tablespoons minced red onions
2 tablespoons minced fresh basil
Taste and adjust the seasonings. Serve at room temperature or slightly chilled.

Tortellini (or Ravioli) Salad

4 to 6 servings

This main-dish pasta salad invites improvisation. Try other combinations of olives, herbs, and cheese for those suggested here.
Toss together gently in a large bowl:
1 pound tortellini or small cheese ravioli, cooked until tender but firm, rinsed with cool water, and drained
2 pounds ripe tomatoes, peeled, seeded, and very coarsely chopped
One 16-ounce jar marinated artichoke hearts, drained and quartered
½ cup Niçoise or other oil-cured black olives, pitted and coarsely chopped
3 tablespoons drained capers (optional)
About 40 small fresh basil leaves, torn into pieces
Season with:
2 to 3 drops red wine vinegar
Salt and ground black pepper to taste
Let cool for several minutes, then add:
4 ounces mozzarella cheese (preferably fresh), cut into ½-inch cubes
Toss again. Serve warm or at room temperature.

Orzo Salad

4 to 6 servings

Orzo is a tiny pasta shaped like large grains of rice. (It is sometimes called riso.) This salad is perfect for buffets, as it can sit out for a while without deteriorating.

Stir together in a medium bowl:

¾ cup minced shallots
½ cup extra-virgin olive oil
2 tablespoons fresh lemon juice
1 clove garlic, minced
½ teaspoon finely grated lemon zest, or more to taste
Ground black pepper to taste

Add while still warm and toss:

8 ounces orzo pasta (1 cup uncooked), cooked until tender but firm and drained

Let cool to room temperature, then stir in:

1 small cucumber, seeded and finely diced
½ yellow or red bell pepper, finely diced
½ cup crumbled ricotta salata or feta cheese
¼ cup minced fresh parsley
1 tablespoon snipped fresh chives
Salt to taste

Let the salad stand for 15 minutes for the flavors to blend. Taste and adjust the seasonings. Serve at room temperature.

RICOTTA SALATA

Imported from central and southern Italy, this salted fresh sheep's milk ricotta is pressed into cylinders that are usually about 7 x 4 inches. It tastes clean, sweet-salty, and fresh. Use ricotta salata wherever a lively, refreshing quality is needed. Shave or crumble it over your favorite salads and pastas, substitute it for feta cheese in recipes, or serve it as an antipasto with roasted peppers, olives, and rustic bread. You can find ricotta salata in some supermarkets and specialty stores.

ABOUT
FISH &
SHELLFISH
SALADS

*N*ot *long ago, seafood salads were among the favorite appetizers in steakhouses and other traditional dining establishments. These refreshing combinations of crisp greens and chilled, cooked fish and shellfish made the ideal start to a meal that usually featured a robust main course. Nowadays, the salads in this chapter are more likely to star as entrées in their own right. That status eloquently expresses the high regard many of us have for light, fresh-tasting foods and for fish and shellfish in particular.*

On the following pages, you'll find a selection of classic recipes, such as Crab Louis and Lobster Salad Vinaigrette, 88, all of which are well suited to be served as supporting or main players on a menu. Accompanying these classics are recipes that reflect contemporary tastes, from a salad of Spinach with Seared Shrimp, Bacon, and Roasted Bell Peppers, 84, to Grilled Swordfish, Tangerine, and Jícama Salad, 87.

For making fish and shellfish salads, there is one simple rule to keep in mind. Use the best-quality fresh seafood you can find, whether from a specialty fishmonger or from a supermarket fish department. The products you buy should be absolutely fresh, with moist flesh, good color, and the clean scent of the sea.

Crab Louis, 88

Salade Niçoise

4 to 6 servings

Cook in a large pot of boiling salted water until tender, about 20 minutes:

6 small red new potatoes

Remove with a slotted spoon, let cool, cut into ½-inch-thick slices, and place in a medium bowl. Meanwhile, add to the pot and boil until bright green but still crisp, 2 to 3 minutes:

1 pound green beans, trimmed

Drain, refresh under cold running water, drain again, and add to the potatoes. Whisk in a small bowl:

3 tablespoons red wine vinegar

2 teaspoons Dijon mustard

Salt and ground black pepper to taste

Add in a slow, steady stream, whisking constantly:

6 tablespoons olive oil, preferably extra virgin

Drizzle about one-quarter of the dressing over the potatoes and beans and gently toss to coat, being careful not to break the potato slices. Arrange on a large platter:

1 head Boston lettuce, separated into leaves, washed, and dried

Arrange on top of the lettuce:

2 large ripe tomatoes, cut into 8 wedges each

Drizzle another quarter of the dressing on top. Arrange the beans and potatoes on the platter along with:

5 *Hard-Boiled Eggs*, right, halved

Place in the center of the salad:

One 6-ounce can tuna, preferably oil packed, drained and flaked

Drizzle the remaining dressing over all. Scatter over the top:

½ cup Niçoise olives

¼ cup minced fresh parsley

2 to 4 anchovy fillets, rinsed and patted dry (optional)

2 tablespoons drained capers

Salt and ground black pepper to taste

Serve immediately.

Hard-Boiled Eggs

Bring to a boil in a saucepan over high heat:

2 to 4 quarts water, enough to cover eggs by 1 inch

Gently lower into the water with a slotted spoon:

Unshelled eggs

Return the water to a boil and reduce the heat to a simmer. Allow 12 minutes for small and medium, 14 minutes for large, and 15 minutes for extra-large and jumbo eggs. Plunge hard-boiled eggs into cold water to prevent further cooking.

Spinach with Seared Shrimp, Bacon, and Roasted Bell Peppers

4 servings

Roast, 79:

2 bell peppers, preferably 1 each red and yellow

Peel, seed, and cut into thin strips. Heat in a medium skillet over medium heat until hot but not smoking:

2 tablespoons olive oil

Add:

1 pound medium shrimp, shelled and deveined, with tails left on

Salt and ground black pepper to taste

Cook, stirring, until the shrimp have a little color on the outside and are opaque throughout, 3 to 4 minutes each side. Remove from the pan, let cool, and chill. Meanwhile, return the skillet to the heat and cook until crisp, 6 to 8 minutes:

8 slices bacon

Drain on paper towels and coarsely crumble. Whisk together in a small bowl:

¼ cup sherry vinegar

1 tablespoon Dijon mustard

1 tablespoon chopped shallots

1 teaspoon chopped fresh thyme

½ to 1 teaspoon red pepper flakes

Add in a slow, steady stream, whisking constantly:

¾ cup olive oil

Combine the peppers, shrimp, and bacon in a salad bowl with:

4 cups bite-sized pieces spinach (preferably baby leaves), washed and dried

Stir the dressing well, add just enough to moisten the ingredients, and toss to coat and combine. Taste and adjust the seasonings. Serve immediately.

Mixed Greens with Grilled Tuna, Leeks, and Tomatoes

4 servings

Prepare a medium-hot charcoal fire. Boil in water to cover just until tender, about 3 minutes:

4 leeks, root ends carefully trimmed (to keep leeks whole), tough greens trimmed, cleaned thoroughly

Drain, refresh in ice water, and drain again. Meanwhile, have ready along with the leeks:

Four 1½-inch-thick tuna steaks (about 4 ounces each)

2 large ripe tomatoes, cored and cut into 1-inch-thick slices

Lightly brush the leeks, tuna, and tomatoes with:

Olive oil

Sprinkle with:

Salt and ground black pepper to taste

Grill the tuna for 4 to 5 minutes each side for medium-rare. Grill the leeks cut side down for 4 minutes and the tomatoes for 2 minutes each side, just until lightly browned. Divide among 4 serving plates:

2 cups bite-sized pieces salad greens (any combination of mizuna, frisée, escarole, or arugula), washed and dried

1 bunch watercress, tough stems trimmed, washed and dried

Arrange the grilled tuna, leeks, and tomatoes on top of the lettuce. Drizzle over the salads:

⅓ to ½ cup *Creamy Caraway Dressing, right*

Sprinkle with:

Snipped fresh chives

Serve immediately.

Creamy Caraway Dressing

About 1⅓ cups

Whisk together in a small bowl:

½ cup fresh lemon juice

½ cup crème fraîche

2 tablespoons caraway seeds, lightly toasted

1 tablespoon whole-grain mustard

1 tablespoon chopped shallots

1 teaspoon chopped fresh thyme

Add in a slow, steady stream, whisking constantly until smooth:

2 tablespoons extra-virgin olive oil

Season with:

Salt and ground black pepper to taste

Use immediately or refrigerate.

Seafood Salad

6 to 8 servings

This elegant salad makes a splendid lunch or dinner.

Stir together well in a large bowl:

½ cup olive oil

¼ cup fresh lemon juice

1½ tablespoons Dijon mustard

1 tablespoon minced garlic

1 tablespoon drained capers

1 red bell pepper, cut into thin strips

6 green olives, pitted and quartered

6 oil-cured black olives, pitted and quartered

¼ cup coarsely chopped fresh parsley

Add and toss well:

1 pound cleaned squid, cooked, bodies cut crosswise into ¼-inch-thick rings, and tentacles separated

12 ounces medium shrimp, cooked, peeled

4 ounces sea scallops, cooked

12 cherrystone clams, cooked and removed from the shells

12 mussels, cooked and removed from the shells

Season with:

Salt and cracked black peppercorns to taste

Let stand at room temperature for at least 30 minutes or up to 1 hour, toss again, and serve.

Grilled Swordfish, Tangerine, and Jícama Salad

4 servings

Tangerines, particularly seedless ones, are excellent in salads.

Prepare a medium-hot charcoal fire. Whisk together in a small bowl:

½ cup olive oil

2 tablespoons fresh lime juice

2 tablespoons red wine vinegar

2 tablespoons coarsely chopped fresh parsley

1 tablespoon Dijon mustard

1½ teaspoons honey

2 teaspoons ground cumin

Salt and cracked black peppercorns to taste

Have ready:

Four 1- to 1½-inch-thick swordfish steaks (8 to 10 ounces each)

Brush with:

4 teaspoons vegetable oil

Sprinkle with:

Salt and ground black pepper to taste

Grill just until opaque in the center, about 5 minutes each side. Combine in a salad bowl:

1 head Boston lettuce, tough outer leaves removed, inner leaves trimmed, washed, dried, and torn into bite-sized pieces

2 tangerines, seeded and separated into sections, 57

1 medium jícama or celery root, peeled and cut into thin strips

1 red bell pepper, thinly sliced

Salt and ground black pepper to taste

Stir the dressing well, add just enough to moisten the ingredients, and toss to coat. Place the swordfish on top, drizzle any remaining dressing over the salad, and serve.

JÍCAMA

The uninspiring appearance of a jícama—like a rough, brown-skinned turnip—belies its sweet, water-crisp, white flesh. Because its flesh holds its color and texture, jícama is a favorite for the salad bowl and raw vegetable tray. Select small to medium tubers that are uniformly hard, heavy for their size, with no sign of shriveling or drying. To prepare jícama, scrub well, then use a sharp stainless-steel paring knife to peel—the thin skin pulls right off. Remove the thin, fibrous layer beneath. Cut into slices, wedges, cubes, or matchsticks. Store jícama unpeeled and unwrapped in the refrigerator crisper.

Grilled Scallop and Fennel Salad

4 servings

Like greens, foods cooked over a live fire have a kind of immediacy, a direct connection to the outdoors, that is particularly welcome during summer months. Here we combine creamy grilled scallops with smoky fennel and slightly bitter arugula, then add an herb vinaigrette to bind it all together.

Prepare a medium-hot charcoal fire. Wash and pat dry:

1 pound sea scallops

Remove the fronds, trim the base, and cut lengthwise into ½-inch-thick slices:

2 fennel bulbs

Sprinkle lightly with:

Olive oil

Salt and ground black pepper to taste

Grill the scallops on one side until the outside is crisp, 2 to 3 minutes. Turn and grill until the other side is crisp and the center is opaque, 2 to 3 minutes more. Grill the fennel just until tender, about 3 minutes each side. Whisk together in a small bowl:

¼ cup fresh lemon juice

1 tablespoon Dijon mustard

1 tablespoon minced shallots

1 tablespoon minced fresh tarragon

1 tablespoon chopped fresh parsley

1 teaspoon chopped fresh thyme

Salt and ground black pepper to taste

Add in a slow, steady stream, whisking constantly:

½ cup olive oil

Combine the scallops and fennel in a salad bowl along with:

4 cups bite-sized pieces arugula or romaine lettuce, washed and dried

1 small red onion, thinly sliced

2 ripe tomatoes, cored and cut into wedges

Stir the dressing well, add just enough to moisten the ingredients, toss to coat, and serve.

Lobster Salad Vinaigrette

4 to 6 servings

This lobster salad (opposite) can also be made with cooked crabmeat or shrimp. It makes an opulent appetizer or can be served as a light main course for lunch or dinner.

Preheat the oven to 425°F.

Toss together on a baking sheet:

6 thick slices French bread, cut into 1-inch cubes

3 tablespoons extra-virgin olive oil

Bake, shaking the pan once or twice, until golden brown, about 10 minutes. Prepare:

Basil Chive Vinaigrette, 108

Combine in a salad bowl:

2 cups watercress, with tender stems, washed and dried

2 cups mesclun or baby romaine leaves, washed and dried

1½ cups thinly sliced Belgian endive, washed and dried

Toss well with just enough vinaigrette to coat the greens. Divide the greens among salad plates.

Toss together, adding just enough vinaigrette to coat:

10 to 12 ounces cooked lobster meat, cut into ½-inch chunks

1 ripe avocado, peeled and diced

½ red bell pepper, diced

½ yellow bell pepper, diced

Spoon the lobster mixture over the greens and garnish with the croutons along with:

2 ripe plum tomatoes, peeled, seeded, and diced

Drizzle more vinaigrette over the salads if desired.

Lobster Salad

2 servings

Combine in a medium bowl:

2 cups chopped or shredded cooked lobster meat

½ cup sour cream, mayonnaise, or yogurt

⅔ cup thinly sliced seeded, peeled cucumber (optional)

1 *Hard-Boiled Egg,* 84, chopped (optional)

Stir in:

3 tablespoons slivered blanched snow peas

1 tablespoon finely snipped fresh chives

1 tablespoon minced fresh parsley

1 teaspoon minced fresh tarragon

1 teaspoon fresh lemon juice

¼ teaspoon grated lemon zest

Serve immediately on chilled plates lined with:

Boston lettuce leaves or mixed greens, washed and dried

Garnish with:

Snipped fresh chives

Lemon wedges

Crab Louis

4 servings

This salad was created by the chef at the Olympic Club in Seattle in the late nineteenth century. The area's renowned Dungeness crabs, no doubt, inspired the original creation.

Arrange on a platter or in a salad bowl:

Boston or Bibb lettuce leaves, washed and dried

Place on top:

About 1 cup thin strips Boston, Bibb, or red-leaf lettuce, washed and dried

Heap on top of these:

2 cups cooked lump crabmeat, preferably fresh, picked over for shell and cartilage

Pour over the crab:

1 cup *Sauce Louis,* right

Garnish with:

2 *Hard-Boiled Eggs,* 84, sliced (optional)

Snipped fresh chives

Serve at once.

Sauce Louis

About 2 cups

Originally created for Crab Louis, left, this dressing is also especially relished with salads that include artichokes, shrimp, or lobster.

Stir together in a small bowl until well blended:

1 cup *Traditional Mayonnaise,* 116, or *Blender Mayonnaise,* 118

¼ cup heavy cream or crème fraîche (optional)

¼ cup chili sauce

¼ cup finely chopped red or yellow bell peppers

¼ cup finely chopped scallions

2 tablespoons fresh lemon juice

1 teaspoon Worcestershire sauce

Salt and ground black pepper to taste

Taste the sauce and adjust the seasonings. Use immediately or cover and refrigerate.

ABOUT **MEAT & POULTRY** SALADS

Almost any combination of leafy greens, vegetables, starches, or even fruits may be mixed with cooked meat or poultry and bound together with a dressing to create a satisfying savory salad. Many meat and poultry salads have become favorite main courses at lunchtime or for a light, warm-weather dinner.

There are no fixed rules for these combinations. In fact, an excess of leftovers or a trip to a farmers' market may inspire some of the best. When improvising, first settle on a dominant ingredient or flavor and then add foods that offer a complementary or contrasting flavor, texture, and appearance.

Leftover chicken or red meat makes an ideal base for these salads. Certainly, if one of the following recipes inspires you, cook fresh poultry or meat expressly for the salad. Many of the other ingredients may also be prepared in advance, but it is best to assemble the salad just before serving in order to distribute the dressing and adjust the seasonings. When lettuce or other leaves are part of the combination, they should always be added at the last possible moment so they remain cool and crisp.

Chinese Chicken Salad, 98

Bistro Salad

6 servings

This classic, known in France as frisée aux lardons, *can be served without the eggs. Thick-cut bacon, which will not need blanching, can be substituted for the salt pork.*

Preheat the oven to 350°F.
Have ready:

10 slices French bread

Sprinkle both sides with:

2 to 3 tablespoons olive oil

Salt and ground black pepper to taste

Cut the bread into ½-inch cubes. Spread on a baking sheet and bake, shaking the pan once or twice, until golden brown, about 10 minutes.

Boil in water to cover for 2 minutes:

8 ounces salt pork, diced

Drain, rinse with cold water, and pat dry. Heat in a skillet over medium heat until hot but not smoking:

1 tablespoon vegetable oil

Add the salt pork and cook, stirring, until browned, 6 to 8 minutes. Remove with a slotted spoon and drain on paper towels. Pour ½ cup of the fat in the skillet into a small bowl and whisk in:

2 shallots, thinly sliced crosswise

3 tablespoons red wine vinegar

1 tablespoon minced fresh parsley

2 cloves garlic, minced

1 teaspoon fresh thyme leaves

Salt and ground black pepper to taste

In a salad bowl, toss the salt pork and croutons with:

2 large heads frisée (curly endive), washed, dried, and torn into bite-sized pieces

Toss well with just enough dressing to coat. Divide among 6 salad plates and top with:

6 large eggs, poached, below, and trimmed

Minced fresh parsley (optional)

Serve immediately.

Poached Eggs

6 servings

In this updated method, poached eggs are held at 150°F for 15 minutes to ensure a perfectly safe egg.

Heat 2 to 3 inches of water in a large saucepan over medium heat until almost boiling. Add:

1 tablespoon vinegar (any type)

Crack into 6 small cups and slide one by one from the cups into the simmering water:

6 eggs

Cook, maintaining the water just below a simmer, until the whites are set and the centers are still soft. Remove with a slotted spoon and set in a second pot of water warmed to 150°F. Cover and let stand for 15 minutes; reheat if the temperature falls below 145°F. Drain each egg with a slotted spoon and hold it against a dry dish towel to absorb as much water as possible.

Salad of Grilled Chicken and Tart Greens

4 to 6 servings

A good way to use up leftover chicken.
Combine in a salad bowl:

10 to 12 cups bite-sized pieces bitter greens (any combination of arugula, escarole, young dandelion greens, curly endive, mizuna, watercress, and radicchio), washed and dried

Refrigerate the greens.
Prepare:

Apricot Dressing, **112, or other fruit-based dressing**

Toss the greens well with just enough dressing to lightly coat. Cut diagonally into 1-inch-thick strips:

2 whole boneless, skinless chicken breasts (about 1¼ pounds), grilled or broiled

Divide the greens among salad plates and arrange the chicken on top. If desired, drizzle more dressing over the salads and serve immediately (opposite).

Sautéed Veal Medallions on Arugula Tomato Salad

4 servings

Whisk together in a small bowl:

¼ cup extra-virgin olive oil
2 tablespoons fresh orange juice
2 tablespoons fresh lemon juice
1 teaspoon grated orange zest
Salt and ground black pepper to taste

Toss together in a large bowl:

6 cups torn arugula leaves, washed and dried
2 medium tomatoes, cored and diced

Position a rack in the lower third of the oven. Preheat the oven to 180°F. Have ready an ovenproof platter.

Pat dry:

8 veal medallions, cut ¾ inch thick from the center loin

Season with:

Salt and ground black pepper to taste

Heat in a large skillet over medium-high heat:

2 tablespoons unsalted butter

Add the medallions in batches, being careful not to crowd the pan, and sear until golden on the bottom, about 2 minutes. Turn and sear the second side. Remove to the platter and keep warm in the oven.

Repeat, adding more butter to the pan as needed, until all the medallions are cooked. Increase the heat to high and add to the skillet:

¼ cup chicken or veal stock

Boil, stirring, until the sauce is syrupy and glazelike, 1 to 2 minutes. Thinly slice the meat. Toss the arugula with the orange dressing and arrange the salad on 4 plates. Divide the veal and arrange it over the salads.

Sprinkle with:

Salt and ground black pepper

Drizzle the pan sauce over the veal. Serve immediately.

Chef's Salad

4 to 6 servings

Place on a large platter:

About 10 cups bite-sized pieces salad greens of your choice, washed and dried

Prepare one of the following salad dressings and add just enough (about ¾ cup) to lightly coat the salad greens:

Basic Vinaigrette, 108, Creamy Blue-Cheese Dressing, 121, or Thousand Island Dressing, 121

Arrange on top, preferably in triangular sections like slices of pizza:

1 cup long, thin strips cooked chicken or turkey breast meat

About 4 ounces smoked or baked ham, cut into long, thin strips, or prosciutto, very thinly sliced and rolled into cigar shapes

About 5 ounces Swiss, Cheddar, Gruyère, or other firm cheese, cut into long, thin strips

Also add:

2 ripe tomatoes, cut into wedges

2 or 3 Hard-Boiled Eggs, 84, quartered lengthwise

12 brine-cured black olives, pitted

Sprinkle with:

½ cup minced fresh parsley

Salt and ground black pepper to taste

Serve immediately.

Chicken or Turkey Salad

4 to 6 servings

For the ultimate chicken or turkey salad, roast the poultry on the bone, let it cool enough to handle, and shred or chop the meat into bite-sized pieces or large chunks. Be sure to include plenty of both dark and light meat for the best flavor.

Combine in a medium bowl:

2 cups diced cooked chicken or turkey

1 cup diced celery

Combine with:

½ to 1 cup mayonnaise

Salt and ground black pepper to taste

Serve on a bed of:

Lettuce leaves

If desired, garnish with:

1 tablespoon chopped fresh parsley or tarragon (optional)

CURRIED CHICKEN OR TURKEY SALAD

Prepare *Chicken or Turkey Salad, left,* replacing the celery with ¼ cup each raisins and chopped toasted walnuts or almonds and 2 chopped scallions. Use *Curry Mayonnaise, 119.*

Poached Chicken

Cook chicken parts or breasts just to the point where they release clear juices when pricked with a fork or small knife, or they will be disappointingly dry and firm.

Place in a Dutch oven:

3½ pounds chicken parts or 1½ pounds boneless, skinless chicken breast or turkey breast cutlets or tenders

Add:

1¾ to 2 cups chicken stock

Pour in just enough water to cover the pieces. Chicken parts may require as much as 3 cups water to be covered, while boneless, skinless breasts may not need any at all. Bring to a simmer over high heat, then reduce the heat so that the poaching liquid barely bubbles. Partially cover and cook until the meat releases clear juices when pierced with a fork, 25 to 30 minutes for chicken parts, 8 to 12 minutes for boneless, skinless chicken or turkey breast. Remove the meat from the stock and let stand until cool enough to handle. If using chicken parts, remove and discard the skin and bones. Cut or shred the meat into bite-sized pieces.

Thai Beef Salad

6 servings

This refreshing, aromatic salad is typical of Thai cooking.

Bring to a boil in a large pot:

12 cups water

Add:

1½ pounds beef tenderloin, trimmed of fat and tied

Cover and cook at a steady simmer for 15 to 18 minutes for medium-rare. Remove the beef, cover with a damp dish towel, and let cool to room temperature. Meanwhile, combine in a salad bowl:

3 bunches watercress, tough stems trimmed, washed and dried
1¼ cups fresh mint leaves
1¼ cups fresh cilantro leaves
2 bunches radishes, thinly sliced
1 medium red onion, thinly sliced
2 tablespoons thin strips lemon zest

Cover and refrigerate until ready to serve. Whisk together in a small bowl:

½ cup vegetable oil
½ cup fresh lime juice
3 tablespoons fish sauce (optional)
1 tablespoon soy sauce
1½ teaspoons sugar
Red pepper flakes to taste
Salt and ground black pepper to taste

Slice the beef tenderloin crosswise ½ inch thick, then cut into ½-inch-thick strips. Add the beef and dressing to the watercress mixture, toss to coat and combine, and serve immediately.

FISH SAUCE

Called nu'o'c ma'm in Vietnam and nam pla in Thailand, fish sauce is made by packing fish, usually anchovies, in crocks or barrels, covering them with brine, and allowing them to ferment in the tropical sun over a period of months. The resulting brown liquid is drained off and used as both a condiment and a flavoring. Like olive oil, the first pressing (in this case, siphoning), from which flows a clear amber liquid, is most highly prized and is usually reserved for dipping sauces. Fish sauce keeps indefinitely on the shelf.

Turkey Salad with Chutney and Cashews

4 servings

This salad is delicious anytime, but it is a particularly good way to use leftover Thanksgiving turkey. You can use your favorite prepared mango chutney or make your own.

Whisk together in a large bowl:

½ cup mayonnaise
½ cup sour cream

3 tablespoons mango chutney, coarsely chopped
2 teaspoons curry powder
Salt and ground black pepper to taste

Add and toss to coat:

3 cups thin strips cooked turkey meat

3 scallions, minced
2 celery stalks, thinly sliced
½ cup coarsely chopped roasted cashews
⅓ cup dried currants

Cover and refrigerate until cold.
If desired, serve on a bed of:

Salad greens, washed and dried

Chinese Chicken Salad

4 servings

Be sure to reserve some of the juice from the mandarin oranges, as it adds a delicious sweet tang to the citrus dressing.

Combine in a large bowl:

4 cups thin strips cooked chicken (about 1 pound cooked)
1 cup canned mandarin oranges, drained, juice reserved
⅔ cup sliced scallions
½ cup chopped roasted unsalted peanuts

Whisk together in a small bowl until well blended:

⅔ cup reserved mandarin orange juice
½ cup peanut oil
2 tablespoons fresh lemon juice
1½ teaspoons chili oil (optional)
1 teaspoon minced peeled fresh ginger
½ teaspoon salt, or to taste
¼ teaspoon ground Szechuan peppercorns

Pour ½ cup dressing over the chicken mixture and toss to combine. Taste and adjust the seasonings. Serve the salad over:

4 cups shredded Chinese (Napa) cabbage

Top with:

½ cup chopped roasted unsalted peanuts
1 cup chow mein noodles

Drizzle the remaining dressing over the salad and serve.

Southwestern Chicken Salad

4 servings

To turn this salad into a snack, omit the bed of cabbage and serve it with corn tortilla chips.

Toss to combine in a large bowl:

2 whole chicken breasts, poached, 96, or baked, skinned, boned, and shredded or diced

1 small red onion, minced

2 ripe plum tomatoes, seeded and diced

1 ripe avocado, pitted, peeled, and diced or sliced

½ cup minced fresh cilantro

¼ cup olive oil

½ teaspoon grated lime zest

¼ cup fresh lime juice

1 teaspoon ground cumin

½ teaspoon chili powder, or to taste

Salt and ground black pepper to taste

Cover and refrigerate for at least 1 hour to allow the flavors to blend. Combine and divide among 4 salad plates:

2 cups finely shredded red cabbage

2 cups finely shredded green cabbage

Top with the chicken salad and sprinkle with:

½ cup coarsely chopped roasted peanuts

Serve immediately.

New Mexican Chili Powder

About ½ cup

Based on ground chilies, this is a blend created to flavor Southwestern dishes. Combine and toast in a skillet over medium heat for 2 minutes:

5 tablespoons ground mild chili peppers, such as New Mexico, pasilla, or ancho

2 tablespoons dried oregano

1½ tablespoons ground cumin

½ teaspoon ground red pepper, or to taste

Cobb Salad

4 to 6 servings

This close cousin (opposite) to Chef's Salad, 96, was created in the mid-1920s by restaurateur Bob Cobb at his Brown Derby Restaurant in Los Angeles.
Mash together in a small bowl until a paste is formed:
1 clove garlic, peeled
¼ teaspoon salt
Whisk in:
⅓ cup red wine vinegar
1 tablespoon fresh lemon juice
¼ cup Roquefort or other blue cheese, crumbled

Salt and ground black pepper to taste
Add in a slow, steady stream, whisking constantly:
⅔ cup olive oil
Line a platter with:
1 head Bibb lettuce, separated into leaves, washed, and dried
Arrange on top of the lettuce leaves:
1 large bunch watercress, tough stems trimmed, washed, dried, and coarsely chopped
1 ripe avocado, peeled and diced

4 to 6 cups diced cooked chicken or turkey breast
6 to 8 slices bacon, cooked until crisp and crumbled
3 *Hard-Boiled Eggs, 84,* diced
3 medium tomatoes, coarsely chopped
¼ cup finely snipped fresh chives
¼ cup crumbled Roquefort or other blue cheese
Lightly drizzle the vinaigrette over the salad and serve, passing the remaining vinaigrette separately.

Reduced-Fat Cobb Salad

6 servings

Whisk together until smooth:
½ cup low-fat mayonnaise
½ cup buttermilk
2 shallots, minced
2 tablespoons minced fresh parsley
1 teaspoon minced fresh tarragon
Salt and ground black pepper to taste
Toss with half of the dressing:
1 small head Bibb lettuce, washed, dried, and shredded

1 cup fresh parsley leaves
1 small bunch watercress, tough stems trimmed, washed, dried, and coarsely chopped
Place the greens on a platter and arrange in rows on top:
1 whole chicken breast, poached, 96, skinned, boned, and shredded
4 plum tomatoes, peeled, seeded, and diced

½ ripe avocado, peeled and diced
¼ cup finely snipped fresh chives
Drizzle the remaining dressing over the salad and sprinkle with:
4 slices turkey bacon, cooked until crisp and crumbled
2 tablespoons finely crumbled Roquefort or other blue cheese
Serve immediately.

Taco Salad

4 to 6 servings

This somewhat unusual salad— basically a taco taken apart and reassembled in salad form—is very tasty made with chorizo, ground beef, grilled chicken, or roast pork. Romaine lettuce can be substituted for the iceberg.
Cook, stirring, in a skillet over medium heat until well browned, 5 to 7 minutes:

1 pound chorizo sausage, cut into bite-sized pieces, or 1 pound ground beef seasoned with ground cumin, salt, and pepper
Drain and set aside. Combine in a salad bowl:
1 head iceberg lettuce, washed, dried, and thinly sliced
2 large ripe tomatoes, coarsely chopped

3 scallions, coarsely chopped, or 1 medium onion, diced
1 pound Cheddar cheese, shredded
1 cucumber, peeled, seeded, and diced (optional)
15 ounces taco chips, broken into bite-sized pieces
Add the browned meat along with:
1 cup store-bought tomato salsa
Toss well and serve.

Sandwich Salads

Main-dish ingredients such as egg, tuna, and ham become rich-tasting salad mixtures when chopped, minced, or flaked and then combined with mayonnaise, seasonings, and other embellishments. They are equally at home served as a main-course salad on a bed of greens, stuffed inside a hollowed-out tomato or bell pepper, or scooped atop an avocado half. They can also be used as a sandwich filling between two slices of bread or inside a bun or roll.

Egg Salad

4 servings

Combine in a medium bowl:
6 Hard-Boiled Eggs, 84, finely chopped
¼ to ⅓ cup mayonnaise
2 tablespoons minced onions (optional)
2 tablespoons minced celery (optional)
Salt and ground black pepper to taste
Pinch of curry powder (optional)
Refrigerate until cold.

Tuna Salad

4 servings

Flake with a fork into a medium bowl:
One 6-ounce can water-packed tuna, drained, or 1 cup leftover grilled, poached, or sautéed tuna
Add and stir together well:
½ cup diced celery or diced seeded, peeled cucumber
¼ cup mayonnaise, or to taste
1 tablespoon drained capers (optional)
1 tablespoon minced fresh parsley (optional)
1 teaspoon fresh lemon juice
Salt and ground black pepper to taste
Refrigerate until cold.

Ham Salad

4 servings

Combine in a bowl:
2 cups finely chopped, fully cooked ham
3 Hard-Boiled Eggs, 84, finely chopped (optional)
2 tablespoons minced onions
¼ cup sweet-and-sour pickles, finely chopped
⅓ to ½ cup mayonnaise
1 tablespoon lemon juice (optional)
½ teaspoon yellow or Dijon mustard
Refrigerate until cold.

ABOUT **SALAD** DRESSINGS

A salad dressing is best described as an uncooked sauce and, like all sauces, its role is to enhance the flavor of the food. The dressing can be plain or fancy—as simple as a squeeze of citrus juice or dash of vinegar and a splash of oil, or as complex as an emulsion of oil and acid flavored with herbs, spices, chives or shallots, eggs, stock or vegetable juice, even such weighty substances as relish, salsa, chutney, tapenade, or pesto.

Whatever its style, however, a well-made salad dressing is a balancing act. It should possess a distinct character but never steal the show. A dressing should be well seasoned (typically with a tang of acidity to deliver zest to the food) but not so assertive that it overwhelms the taste of the more delicate salad. And, finally, a salad dressing should have enough body to lightly coat the salad but never be so heavy that the greens collapse under its weight. Before using any dressing, taste it on a lettuce leaf or other element of the salad itself and adjust the seasonings and consistency as necessary.

Clockwise from top left: *Fresh Herb Vinaigrette, 108; Classic Russian Dressing, 121; Ranch Dressing, 122; Green Goddess Dressing, 121; Lemon Caper Vinaigrette, 108 (center)*

Making a Vinaigrette

While the ingredients in a vinaigrette are few and quite simple—three to four parts oil (usually olive) and one part acid (usually wine vinegar), seasoned with salt and pepper and often spiced with mustard and/or garlic—the technique for combining them requires a bit of understanding. Left alone, the elements in a simple vinaigrette do not mix—they separate—making it difficult to dress a salad evenly. The oil rises to the top and the vinegar, which behaves like water, sinks to the bottom. To create a dressing with an even distribution of oil and vinegar, the two elements must be combined in some sort of an emulsion, meaning that the two repellent ingredients become mixed.

The most surefire way to make a thick, well-emulsified vinaigrette is to first whisk together the vinegar or lemon juice and the seasonings (salt, minced shallots or other members of the onion tribe, and mustard) in a small bowl. Then slowly add the oil, drop by drop, whisking as you go, until the dressing begins to thicken. Add the oil in more of a steady stream as the dressing becomes noticeably thicker. An alternative technique is to place the vinegar or lemon juice and seasonings in a small jar with a tight-fitting lid and shake to blend. Then add the oil in three or four additions, shaking vigorously between additions. A third and equally popular method is to mix the vinegar and seasonings in a blender and then add the oil in a slow, steady stream with the machine running.

Vinaigrette can be stored, tightly covered, in the refrigerator for up to 2 weeks. Always whisk dressings briskly just before adding them to salads so that the ingredients are well mixed and in balance, and don't add more vinaigrette than is necessary to lightly coat the salad.

Oil and Acid

Although the ingredients in a vinaigrette are ordinary—oil and acid—the flavor possibilities are extraordinary, thanks to the abundant variety of oils and vinegars available to us. The salad oil par excellence is extravirgin olive oil, but this varies greatly in both quality and character, depending on the place of origin and the producer. We recommend you sample as many oils as possible (specialty food stores sometimes offer tastings) to find one you like. Oil labeled simply "virgin" (without the "extra") is rarely seen in the United States but is usually fine for salad dressing. Pure olive oil, less delicate in flavor and higher in acidity, is generally preferred for cooking rather than dressing.

In multi-ingredient dressings, you may wish to avoid olive oil altogether and use a less expensive and more neutral-tasting oil, such as canola, corn, peanut, sunflower, or safflower. On the other hand, for certain salads, such strongly flavored oils as walnut, almond, hazelnut, and toasted sesame oil are appropriate. Since nut oils tend to be very assertive, temper them by adding only a few tablespoons to a dressing and filling out the remainder with a more neutral oil.

Vinegars vary greatly in acidity and in flavor, and different types will have different effects on your dressing. Again, let your nose and palate be your guide to find what you like. Wine vinegar, the most readily available kind, is most popular for salad dressings. The most complex and flavorful wine vinegar is that made in Spain from sherry; it has high acidity and a very strong, robust flavor—richer, nuttier, and more complex than that of other wine vinegars—and has long been a favorite vinegar of good cooks.

As for the popular balsamic vinegar, if you find one you like, by all means blend a bit of it into salad dressings as a seasoning. If you are lucky enough to come into possession of some true *aceto balsamico tradizionale*—it can cost a hundred dollars or more for a few ounces—please don't use it in salad dressing! Drizzle a few drops over cooked asparagus, over a simply grilled piece of fish or meat, or on shards of Parmigiano-Reggiano.

Citrus juice makes a good alternative to vinegar in salad dressings. Lemon juice is the most versatile, but for certain dressings, lime, orange, or even grapefruit juice might be appropriate. Bear in mind that citrus juice is less acidic than most vinegar, which means that you can make dressing with a ratio closer to two parts oil to one part acid. Some cooks like to combine a bit of lemon juice and a bit of vinegar. With its lower acidity, a salad dressed with citrus juice is more "wine friendly" than one dressed with vinegar.

Other Ingredients

Beyond the use of different oils and vinegars, there are countless ways to create distinctive and delicious salad dressings. As more flavorings and ingredients take center stage, the dressing loses the strict character of an oil-and-vinegar-based vinaigrette. These dressings add textural interest as well as flavor to a salad. Here is a list of some of our favorite additions:

Herbs: Finely chopped or pureed. Dressings made with hearty herbs such as rosemary and oregano should be allowed to sit for several hours for the flavors to infuse.

Assertive Ingredients: Chopped olives, pickles, anchovies, capers, mustard, tapenade, pesto, relish, and garlic. Use these with care in dressings made with flavorful oils because their flavors may clash. Too many assertive flavors in one dressing will cancel each other out.

Wine and Spirits: A splash of good-quality red or white wine or spirits, such as port, whiskey, or brandy, adds an exciting dimension to a basic vinaigrette.

Fruit or Vegetable Purees and Juices: Purees add flavor, body, and visual appeal to dressings. Be sure to squeeze any excess water from the puree first. Vegetable and fruit juices are also used but may result in a thinner dressing.

Cheese: Soft and crumbly cheeses can be blended into the vinegar. Hard cheese should be grated first.

Sweeteners: Honey, maple syrup, pomegranate juice, and molasses. A touch of sweet nicely balances some salads, but don't overdo it.

Basic Vinaigrette or French Dressing

About 1 ½ cups

Vinaigrette is the preferred dressing in France for green salads, avocados, artichokes, and many kinds of sliced, shredded, or chopped vegetables. It is also the starting point for a host of more complicated dressings and accepts a variety of accents with additional ingredients. The optional ingredients in this recipe not only add flavor but also help maintain the emulsion of oil and vinegar essential to a good vinaigrette.

If garlic flavor is desired, mash together with the back of a spoon until a paste is formed:

1 small clove garlic, peeled
2 to 3 pinches of salt

Remove to a small bowl or a jar with a tight-fitting lid. Add and whisk or shake until well blended:

⅓ to ½ cup red wine vinegar or fresh lemon juice
1 shallot, minced

1 teaspoon Dijon mustard (optional)
Salt and ground black pepper to taste

Add in a slow, steady stream, whisking constantly, or add to the jar and shake until smooth:

1 cup extra-virgin olive oil

Taste and adjust the seasonings. Use at once or cover and refrigerate.

Reduced-Fat Vinaigrette

About 1 ½ cups

This recipe uses chicken stock to replace much of the oil. While this dressing will never be as emulsified as a standard vinaigrette, it is much lower in calories.

Whisk together in a small bowl or shake in a jar with a tight-fitting lid:

3 tablespoons red wine vinegar or fresh lemon juice
1 tablespoon Dijon mustard
1 clove garlic, minced
Salt and ground black pepper to taste

Add in a slow, steady stream,

whisking constantly, or add to the jar and shake until smooth:

¾ cup chicken stock
3 tablespoons extra-virgin olive oil

Taste and adjust the seasonings. Use at once or cover and refrigerate.

FRESH HERB VINAIGRETTE

Prepare *Basic Vinaigrette, above,* or *Reduced-Fat Vinaigrette, above,* adding ⅓ cup minced or finely snipped fresh herbs (basil, dill, parsley, chives, and/or thyme).

BASIL CHIVE VINAIGRETTE

Prepare *Basic Vinaigrette, above,* or *Reduced-Fat Vinaigrette, above,* adding ⅓ cup minced fresh basil, ⅓ cup finely snipped fresh chives, and, if desired, 1 tablespoon walnut oil.

GREEN PEPPERCORN VINAIGRETTE

Prepare *Basic Vinaigrette, above,* or

Reduced-Fat Vinaigrette, above, adding 2 tablespoons minced drained green peppercorns or 1 tablespoon cracked dried green peppercorns.

LIME VINAIGRETTE

Prepare *Basic Vinaigrette, above,* or *Reduced-Fat Vinaigrette, above,* substituting ¼ cup fresh lime juice for the vinegar or lemon juice and, if desired, adding a large pinch of toasted cumin seeds.

LEMON CAPER VINAIGRETTE

Prepare *Basic Vinaigrette, above,* or *Reduced-Fat Vinaigrette, above,* with fresh lemon juice and add 1 tablespoon

minced drained capers, 1 tablespoon minced fresh parsley, and ½ teaspoon finely grated lemon zest.

BLACK PEPPER VINAIGRETTE

Prepare *Basic Vinaigrette, above,* or *Reduced-Fat Vinaigrette, above,* adding 1 teaspoon finely grated lemon zest and 2 teaspoons cracked black peppercorns, or to taste.

HORSERADISH VINAIGRETTE

Prepare *Basic Vinaigrette, above,* or *Reduced-Fat Vinaigrette, above,* substituting cider vinegar for the red wine vinegar or lemon juice and adding 1 tablespoon drained horseradish.

OLIVE OIL

The best grades of olive oil are made simply: The fruit is crushed and the oil collected. Pressing is done from mid-autumn to January, depending upon origin. Usually these oils reach the market by early spring. Store in a cool, dark place and use within 1 year. Keep oil away from heat and light.

Many olive oil connoisseurs argue that the best olive oils should merely be drizzled over foods and not mixed into dressings. They claim that whisking or vigorous blending destroys the fruity, delicate character of extra-virgin olive oil. We find that the benefits of a good olive oil in a dressing outweigh this claim.

Olive oils are graded according to how much acidity they contain and whether they are processed with or without solvents. As yet, the United States has no standard for imported Italian oils.

Extra-Virgin Olive Oil: These oils are pressed and processed without heat or solvents. Color is no indication of quality and ranges from gold to deep green, depending upon where and with what olives the oil is made. Clouded, unfiltered oils are prized by many for their sometimes fuller flavor. Lamentably the words "extra virgin" on the bottle do not guarantee good-tasting oil. If at all possible, sample before buying any quantity.

Fine Virgin Olive Oil: Pressed and processed without heat or chemicals. It has a flavor and character more subdued than extra-virgin oil.

Olive Oil: Replaces what used to be called "pure olive oil." This oil is refined with solvents or chemicals, which are steamed off. It will gain color and flavor from blending with virgin olive oil.

Honey Mustard Vinaigrette

About ¾ cup

This vinaigrette, in which honey balances the bite of whole-grain mustard, is delicious tossed with vegetable-laden green salads or potato or bean combinations.

Whisk together in a small bowl or shake in a jar with a tight-fitting lid:

2 tablespoons fresh lemon juice
1 tablespoon white wine vinegar
1 teaspoon honey, or to taste
1 teaspoon whole-grain mustard, or to taste

Salt and ground black pepper to taste

Add in a slow, steady stream, whisking constantly, or add to the jar and shake until smooth:

6 tablespoons extra-virgin olive oil

Taste and adjust the seasonings. Use the vinaigrette immediately or cover and refrigerate.

Tomato Mint Vinaigrette

About 2 cups

Over six hundred mints have been named, but the true mints we commonly use in cooking are peppermint and spearmint. Any will work in this recipe.

Puree in a food processor until smooth, about 1 minute:

1 ripe tomato, peeled and seeded

Add and process for 15 seconds:

½ cup chopped fresh mint
1 shallot, chopped
2 tablespoons red wine vinegar

2 tablespoons fresh lime juice
1 teaspoon Dijon mustard
1 clove garlic, minced
Salt and ground black pepper to taste

With the machine running, slowly pour through the feed tube and process until smooth:

½ cup olive oil

Taste and adjust the seasonings. Use the vinaigrette immediately or cover and refrigerate.

Spicy Walnut Vinaigrette

About 1 ¼ cups

Whisk together in a small bowl or shake in a jar with a tight-fitting lid:

1 shallot, minced
3 tablespoons balsamic vinegar, or to taste
2 tablespoons minced walnuts
2 teaspoons Dijon mustard
Salt to taste
Hot red pepper sauce to taste

Add in a slow, steady stream, whisking constantly, or add to the jar and shake until smooth:

⅓ cup extra-virgin olive oil
⅓ cup walnut oil

Taste and adjust the seasonings. Use the vinaigrette immediately or cover and refrigerate.

Thai Vinaigrette

About ⅔ cup

In this vinaigrette, the high acidity is balanced by a touch of sweetness.
Whisk together in a small bowl or shake in a jar with a tight-fitting lid:

¼ cup fresh lime juice
2 tablespoons fish sauce
1 teaspoon sugar
Salt to taste
Ground red pepper to taste

Add in a slow, steady stream, whisking constantly, or add to the jar and shake until smooth:

6 tablespoons vegetable oil
Taste and adjust the seasonings. Use the vinaigrette immediately or cover and refrigerate.

SHALLOTS

These are members of the onion family, usually the size of small boiling onions, with copper, gold, or gray-brown skin. The flavor of a shallot is milder than any other onion, but warm and intense.

Fennel Parmesan Vinaigrette

About 1 ½ cups

Whisk together in a small bowl or shake in a jar with a tight-fitting lid:

⅓ cup balsamic vinegar
3 tablespoons grated Parmesan cheese
1 teaspoon fennel seeds, crushed

1 shallot, minced
1 clove garlic, minced
Salt and ground black pepper to taste
Add in a slow, steady stream, whisking constantly, or add to the jar and

shake until smooth:

1 cup olive oil
Taste and adjust the seasonings. Use the vinaigrette immediately or cover and refrigerate.

Ginger Soy Vinaigrette

About 1 cup

This Asian-inspired, slightly spicy dressing is particularly nice with watercress salads.
Mash together until a paste is formed:

1 clove garlic, peeled
2 to 3 pinches of salt
Remove to a small food processor or

a blender. Add and puree:

¼ cup rice vinegar
¼ cup minced shallots
2 tablespoons minced peeled fresh ginger
1 tablespoon soy sauce
½ teaspoon toasted sesame oil
Salt to taste

Hot red pepper sauce to taste
With the machine running, slowly pour through the feed tube and process until smooth:

½ cup peanut or vegetable oil
Taste and adjust the seasonings. Use the vinaigrette immediately or cover and refrigerate.

Chunky Blue-Cheese Vinaigrette

About 1 ⅔ cups

If you like a smoother consistency, crumble the cheese more finely.
Whisk together in a small bowl:

¼ cup cider vinegar
¼ cup coarsely chopped fresh parsley

6 dashes of Worcestershire sauce
Salt and ground black pepper to taste
Add in a slow, steady stream, whisking constantly, until smooth:

¾ cup olive oil

Whisk in:

⅓ cup coarsely crumbled blue cheese
Taste and adjust the seasonings. Use the vinaigrette immediately or cover and refrigerate.

Roasted Garlic Dressing

About 1 cup

Preheat the oven to 400°F.
Place on a piece of heavy-duty aluminum foil:

1 head garlic, top third cut off and loose papery peel removed
2 shallots, loose papery peel removed

Sprinkle with:

2 tablespoons olive oil

Wrap and seal the garlic and shallots together tightly. Roast for 1 hour. Remove the package from the oven, open carefully, and let the contents cool. When cool enough to handle, squeeze the garlic and the shallots from their peels into a small food processor or a blender. Add and puree:

2 tablespoons extra-virgin olive oil
1 tablespoon fresh lemon juice
1 tablespoon white wine vinegar
1 teaspoon Dijon mustard
1 teaspoon fresh thyme leaves
1 teaspoon minced fresh rosemary
Salt and ground black pepper to taste

With the machine running, slowly pour through the feed tube and process until smooth:

6 tablespoons olive oil

Taste and adjust the seasonings. Use immediately or cover and refrigerate.

Poppy Seed Honey Dressing

About ⅔ cup

This dressing is an old favorite for salads that combine greens and fruit.
Whisk together in a small bowl or shake in a jar with a tight-fitting lid until smooth:

¼ cup honey
3 tablespoons cider vinegar or other fruit vinegar

2 tablespoons olive oil
1 small shallot, minced
2 teaspoons Dijon mustard
1 teaspoon poppy seeds
Salt and ground black pepper to taste

Taste and adjust the seasonings. Use immediately or cover and refrigerate.

Apricot Dressing

About 1 ½ cups

Whisk together in a medium bowl or shake in a jar with a tight-fitting lid until smooth:

¼ cup apricot nectar
3 tablespoons balsamic vinegar
3 tablespoons minced dried apricots
3 tablespoons coarsely chopped fresh parsley
2 teaspoons minced garlic

2 teaspoons whole-grain mustard
1 teaspoon sugar
Salt and cracked black peppercorns to taste

Add in a slow, steady stream, whisking constantly, or add to the jar and shake until smooth:

¼ cup olive oil

Taste and adjust the seasonings. Use immediately or cover and refrigerate.

Tangerine Shallot Dressing

About 1½ cups

This dressing (above, left) is especially good on any salad with chicken or even just drizzled over grilled chicken.
Mash together until a paste is formed:

1 clove garlic, peeled
2 to 3 pinches of salt

Remove to a small bowl or a jar with a tight-fitting lid. Add and whisk or shake until well blended:

¼ cup fresh tangerine or
    clementine juice
2 tablespoons fresh lemon juice
2 small shallots, minced

Add in a slow, steady stream, whisking constantly, or add to the jar and shake until smooth:

⅔ cup vegetable oil
Taste and adjust the seasonings. Use the dressing immediately or cover and refrigerate.

Sun-Dried Tomato Dressing

About ¾ cup

This simple dressing (above, right) works well on salads that include arugula. It also makes an excellent simple pasta sauce. Try it on cooked spaghettini or small pasta shapes.
With the food processor running, drop through the feed tube and process until finely chopped:

2 small shallots, quartered

1 or 2 cloves garlic, halved
Stop the machine, add, and process until finely minced:

6 sun-dried tomato halves in oil,
    drained and coarsely chopped
6 brine-cured black olives, pitted
2 tablespoons balsamic vinegar
1 tablespoon fresh thyme leaves or
    chopped fresh basil

Salt and ground black pepper
    to taste
With the machine running, slowly pour through the feed tube and process until smooth:

½ cup olive oil
Taste and adjust the seasonings. Use the dressing immediately or cover and refrigerate.

Creamy Dressings

Although the versatility and relative ease of making a vinaigrette is hard to beat, many cooks prefer a thicker, more stable emulsion that doesn't separate as quickly when left to stand, allowing time to attend to other parts of the meal. Adding other ingredients to the vinegar—such as mustard, garlic, onions, pureed vegetables, olive paste, or cream, to name a few—helps to thicken a salad dressing and make the emulsion more stable. These additional ingredients also allow more room to stray away from the classic three-to-one or four-to-one oil-to-vinegar ratio. Apart from vinaigrette-based dressings, creamy-style dressings typically get their thick, smooth consistency not from an oil and vinegar emulsion but from some element that easily produces a smooth, thick consistency—for instance, mayonnaise, yogurt, buttermilk, sour cream, crème fraîche, heavy cream, or tahini.

Like a good vinaigrette, the key to making a good creamy dressing is balance. In every instance acid, be it vinegar or citrus juice, balances the creamy element. In the case of buttermilk, the cook finds acidity and creaminess all in one.

Clockwise from top: Sour cream, heavy cream, yogurt

Midwestern Cream Dressing

About ¾ cup

Whisk together in a small bowl:

¼ cup cider vinegar or white wine vinegar

¼ cup sugar

2 tablespoons light cream

2 teaspoons celery seeds or poppy seeds

Salt and cracked black peppercorns to taste

Taste and adjust the seasonings. Use immediately or cover and refrigerate.

Sour Cream Dressing for Vegetable Salads

About 1 ¼ cups

This easy to prepare recipe can be used as a traditional salad dressing, or it can be served as a dip with seasonal cut vegetables, fresh breadsticks, or potato chips. If you prefer a reduced-fat version, simply substitute low-fat sour cream or low-fat yogurt in place of the full-fat sour cream.

Whisk in a small bowl until smooth:

1 cup sour cream

Stir in:

2 tablespoons minced red bell peppers

1 teaspoon celery seeds or dill seeds

1 teaspoon grated onions

Salt and ground black pepper to taste

Taste and adjust the seasonings. Use immediately or cover and refrigerate.

HOW TO MINCE SHALLOTS

The flesh of shallots can react badly to rough handling. When crushed, it exudes liquid, which may result in the flavor of the shallot going bitter. So mince with care.

1 Sometimes what appears to be one round shallot is two half rounds; pull them apart and set each half on its flat side. Trim off the stem end with a small, sharp knife; leave the root end intact. Pull off the skin.

2 Lay the shallot flat side down. Make parallel cuts lengthwise through the shallot, cutting up to but not through the root end.

3 Depending on the size of the shallot, make 2 to 4 parallel horizontal cuts up to but not through the root.

4 Steady the shallot at the root end. Thinly slice through the shallot at right angles to the previous cuts, making finely minced pieces.

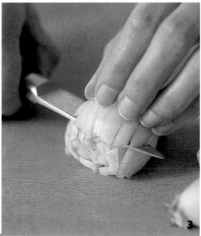

Homemade Mayonnaise

If you are accustomed to store-bought mayonnaise, your first taste of homemade will be a surprise. Homemade mayonnaise is an elegant French sauce. It is also often used as a dressing for salads and as a creamy element in salad dressings. The flavor is bright with lemon juice or vinegar and nutty with good oil. Homemade mayonnaise is elegant and can be made quickly.

Mayonnaise, like vinaigrette, is an emulsion—a stable liquid mixture in which one liquid, egg yolks, is suspended in tiny globules throughout another, oil.

The oil you choose will be the predominant flavor in your mayonnaise. Made entirely with a robust olive or walnut oil, the sauce will suit equally full-flavored ingredients—meats and aromatic vegetables, for example. For delicate ingredients such as fish, a milder oil is recommended. When mayonnaise is to be the base for other flavors, make it with mild-tasting peanut, safflower, grape-seed, or corn oil. For general use, a balance of fruity and mild oils is most satisfying. Usually three parts mild to one part fruity oils is about right. The oil must be very fresh. One tinge of rancidity, and the sauce is all but inedible, so taste the oil before you start. The eggs must also be very fresh; as eggs age, they lose their ability to stabilize an emulsion.

Making mayonnaise in a food processor or blender or with an electric mixer is practically fool-proof, and the sauce has greater volume and a fluffier texture than when made by hand. For the silkiest texture of all, make the sauce by hand.

Ingredients at room temperature emulsify more readily than cold ones, so start by covering the eggs in their shells with hot water to warm them briefly. If the oil was refrigerated, warm to room temperature. To be certain of success when improvising your own formula, bear in mind that 1 egg yolk can emulsify up to about ¾ cup oil, no more. One-half cup is even safer.

Problems with mayonnaise are simple to fix. If the mayonnaise starts to separate, place a fresh egg yolk in a small clean bowl. Slowly add the separated mayonnaise, drizzling it and whisking it in as you first did with the oil. You may need to add more oil to compensate for the extra yolk. If the mayonnaise is too thick for your taste, thin it with a little water or cream.

Homemade mayonnaise can be kept, tightly covered in the refrigerator, for a day or two, but it will lose some of its sheen after a few hours. Mayonnaise does not freeze well. When serving homemade mayonnaise and all foods containing it, keep track of the time it spends outside the refrigerator. Because raw egg contains micro-organisms that start multiplying above 40°F, the maximum time mayonnaise should be out of the refrigerator is 2 hours—and when the air temperature is 85°F or above, it is 1 hour. See also *Egg Safety*, 23.

Traditional Mayonnaise

About 1 cup

Whisk together in a medium bowl until smooth and light:

2 large egg yolks
1 to 2 tablespoons fresh lemon juice or white wine vinegar
¼ teaspoon salt
Pinch of ground white pepper

Whisk in by drops until the mixture starts to thicken and stiffen:

1 cup vegetable oil, at room temperature

As the sauce begins to thicken— when about one-third of the oil has been added—whisk in the oil more steadily, making sure each addition is thoroughly blended before adding the next. Should the oil stop being absorbed, whisk vigorously before adding more. Stir in:

Up to 1½ teaspoons Dijon mustard
Salt and ground black pepper to taste

Serve immediately or refrigerate in a covered jar for 1 to 2 days.

FLAVORING MAYONNAISE

Mayonnaise can be flavored in many ways. Add herbs, dried spices, flavored vinegars, and dry mustard to the yolks at the start. Though lemon juice and wine vinegar are classic, other citrus juices and most other vinegars can also be used. If you know you will be adding liquid flavorings, use extra oil to make an extra-thick sauce.

HOW TO MAKE MAYONNAISE

This is the method for basic mayonnaise, both traditional (by hand) or by food processor or blender. With this mayonnaise, all the variations listed in the pages to follow can be prepared. It can be whisked to a lighter consistency by gradually adding a little water, cream, an appropriately flavored stock, vegetable juice, or even a spirit.

1 Submerge the eggs in warm water to bring them to room temperature.

2 Use a medium ceramic, glass, or stainless-steel bowl (not aluminum or copper, which will react with the acid). Whisk the egg yolks, lemon juice or vinegar, and seasonings until smooth and light.

3 Whisk in a little of the oil by drops until the mixture begins to thicken and stiffen.

4 As the sauce begins to thicken, whisk in the oil more steadily, making sure each addition is thoroughly blended before adding the next.

5 Whisk in the mustard if using and taste and adjust the seasonings.

6 It is easy to fix mayonnaise that separates or breaks. Start by placing an egg yolk in a clean bowl. Then, in a slow steady stream, begin drizzling in the separated mayonnaise, whisking it into the egg yolk as you go. This is, in essence, the same process as adding oil to egg yolks—making mayonnaise. It will create a new emulsification. In addition to the the separated mayonnaise, you may need to whisk in additional oil to compensate for the extra yolk. If the mayonnaise is too thick for your taste, correct it as described above.

Blender Mayonnaise

About 1 cup

If using a food processor, use the plastic blade if you have one, as it seems to make a slightly lighter sauce. Egg white is needed in machine-made mayonnaise. Beat 1 egg well with a fork to blend the yolk and white, let it settle a few seconds, then measure. This recipe can be doubled, in which case, just use 1 large egg.

Combine in a blender or food processor:

2 tablespoons well-beaten egg
1 large egg yolk
¼ teaspoon dry or Dijon mustard

Process on high speed until well blended, about 5 seconds in a blender, 15 seconds in a food processor fitted with the plastic blade, 30 seconds in a food processor fitted with the steel blade. Scrape down the sides, then sprinkle the mixture with:

1 teaspoon fresh lemon juice and/or white wine vinegar or rice vinegar
¼ teaspoon salt

Process for about 2 minutes in a blender, 15 seconds in a food processor fitted with the plastic blade, 7 to 8 seconds in a food processor fitted with the steel blade. Have ready in a small spouted measuring pitcher:

¾ cup oil, at room temperature

With the machine running, add the oil in the thinnest possible stream. After about one-third of the oil has been added—the mixture will have swollen and stiffened—add the oil in a slightly thicker stream. Stop the machine when all has been added and scrape down the sides and around the blade, mixing in any unabsorbed oil. If you want a thicker sauce, add as before:

Up to ¼ cup oil, at room temperature

Should the sauce be too thick, add as needed:

Light or heavy cream, milk, or water, at room temperature

Taste the mayonnaise and stir in:

1½ to 3 teaspoons fresh lemon juice or white wine vinegar
½ to 1 teaspoon dry or Dijon mustard
Salt and ground white pepper to taste

Serve immediately, or refrigerate in a covered jar for 1 to 2 days.

Mayonnaise with Green Herbs

About 1 cup

Fresh herbs vary in intensity, so be sure to add the herbs judiciously to this mayonnaise. Store bunches of fresh herbs in the refrigerator, and make sure their stems are in water. This mayonnaise is excellent served cold with shellfish, vegetables, and cold poached meat.

Prepare Traditional Mayonnaise, 116, or Blender Mayonnaise, above, and stir in:

2 to 3 tablespoons minced fresh herbs, such as tarragon, basil, chervil, chives, parsley, and oregano

Season to taste with:

Salt and ground black pepper

Yogurt Mayonnaise

About 1½ to 2 cups

A tangy light sauce to use in all the ways you would use mayonnaise. For a reduced-fat mayonnaise, use up to 1 cup nonfat yogurt. If you're not concerned about calories but still want the tang, use low-fat or full-fat yogurt. We use white pepper in this mayonnaise, which is often the preferred pepper for light-colored foods.

Prepare Traditional Mayonnaise, 116, or Blender Mayonnaise, above, and add:

½ to 1 cup yogurt (nonfat, low-fat, or full-fat is fine)

Whisk until completely blended. Season to taste with:

Salt and ground white pepper

Chipotle Pepper Mayonnaise

About 1¼ cups

Chipotle peppers (dried smoked jalapeños) show up everywhere, from canned tomato sauce (adobo) to salsas, sauces, pickles, stews, soups, and more. This mayonnaise makes a zesty sauce for meat and poultry.

Prepare Traditional Mayonnaise, 116, or Blender Mayonnaise, opposite, and stir in:

1 tablespoon minced canned chipotle peppers
1 teaspoon minced garlic
1 tablespoon tomato puree
2 tablespoons chopped fresh cilantro
2 tablespoons fresh lime juice

Season to taste with:

Salt and ground black pepper

Curry Mayonnaise

About 1¼ cups

Hoping to export to England the flavors they had enjoyed in India, the British likely took back with them one of the Southern Indian spice mixtures. Use with cold vegetables, eggs, fish, poultry, and meats.

Prepare Traditional Mayonnaise, 116, Blender Mayonnaise, opposite, or Yogurt Mayonnaise, opposite, and set aside. In a small skillet, add:

2 tablespoons best-quality curry powder
2 tablespoons mild-tasting oil

Stir over low heat for 30 to 60 seconds—until you start to smell it. Let cool and whisk into the mayonnaise—Yogurt Mayonnaise is especially good. Season to taste with:

Salt and ground black pepper

Garlic Mayonnaise (Aïoli)

About 1 cup

Sometimes called beurre de Provence—*the butter of Provence—aïoli is traditionally served slightly chilled. Aïoli is a contraction of the Provençal words for garlic and oil.*

Whisk together in a medium bowl until smooth and light:

2 large egg yolks
4 to 6 cloves garlic, finely minced
Salt and ground white pepper to taste

Whisk in by drops until the mixture starts to thicken and stiffen.

1 cup olive oil, or part olive and part safflower or peanut oil, at room temperature

As the sauce begins to thicken, whisk in the oil more steadily, making sure each addition is thoroughly blended before adding the next. Gradually whisk in:

1 teaspoon fresh lemon juice, or to taste
½ teaspoon cold water

Taste and adjust the seasonings. Serve immediately or refrigerate in a jar for 1 to 2 days.

Sauce Rémoulade

About 1½ cups

The French classic.

Prepare Traditional Mayonnaise, 116, or Blender Mayonnaise, opposite, and stir in:

1 Hard-Boiled Egg, 84, finely chopped
1 tablespoon drained capers
1 tablespoon minced cornichons or sour gherkins
1 tablespoon chopped fresh parsley
1½ teaspoons chopped fresh tarragon
1 small clove garlic, minced
½ teaspoon Dijon mustard

Season to taste with:

Salt and ground black pepper

Classic Russian Dressing

About 1¾ cups

An American invention despite its name, this dressing goes well with composed salads.

Stir together in a small bowl until well blended:

1 cup Traditional Mayonnaise, 116, or Blender Mayonnaise, 118

¼ cup chili sauce or tomato ketchup
1 tablespoon freshly grated horseradish
1 teaspoon Worcestershire sauce
1 tablespoon minced fresh parsley (optional)

1 teaspoon grated onions
Salt and ground black pepper to taste

Taste and adjust the seasonings. Use immediately or cover and refrigerate.

Thousand Island Dressing

About 1½ cups

An obvious relative of Russian dressing, Thousand Island is great on a wedge of iceberg lettuce.

Stir together in a small bowl until well blended:

1 cup Traditional Mayonnaise, 116, or Blender Mayonnaise, 118

¼ cup chili sauce or tomato ketchup
1 Hard-Boiled Egg, 84, chopped
2 tablespoons minced gherkins or pickle relish
1 tablespoon minced fresh onions
1 tablespoon minced fresh parsley

1 tablespoon finely snipped fresh chives
Salt and ground black pepper to taste

Taste and adjust the seasonings. Use immediately or cover and refrigerate.

Green Goddess Dressing

About 2 cups

This creamy, herby dressing was invented at the historic Palace Hotel in San Francisco in the 1920s in honor of William Archer's hit play The Green Goddess.

Stir together in a small bowl until well blended:

1 cup Traditional Mayonnaise, 116, or Blender Mayonnaise, 118
½ cup sour cream
¼ cup snipped fresh chives or minced scallions
¼ cup minced fresh parsley
1 tablespoon fresh lemon juice

1 tablespoon white wine vinegar
3 anchovy fillets, rinsed, patted dry, and minced
Salt and ground black pepper to taste

Taste and adjust the seasonings. Use immediately or cover and refrigerate.

Creamy Blue-Cheese Dressing

About 2 cups

Good-quality blue cheese, such as Roquefort, turns this into a truly distinctive dressing.

Puree in a food processor or blender until smooth:

1 cup Traditional Mayonnaise, 116, or Blender Mayonnaise, 118

½ cup sour cream
¼ cup finely chopped fresh parsley
1 to 2 tablespoons fresh lemon juice or red wine vinegar
1 teaspoon minced garlic
6 dashes of Worcestershire sauce
Pinch of ground red pepper

Salt and ground black pepper to taste

Add and process to the desired consistency:

4 ounces blue cheese

Taste and adjust the seasonings. Use immediately or cover and refrigerate.

Clockwise from top: Ranch Dressing, 122; Thousand Island Dressing, above; Green Goddess Dressing, above

Ranch Dressing

About 1 cup

The original version of this now-ubiquitous condiment was created at the Hidden Valley Guest Ranch in Santa Barbara in the 1950s. The term "ranch" has become a generic name not just for a dressing but for a buttermilky flavor. If you prefer a thicker dressing, stir in ⅓ to ½ cup mayonnaise or sour cream.

Mash together until a paste is formed:

1 clove garlic, peeled
2 to 3 pinches of salt

Remove to a small bowl or a jar with a tight-fitting lid. Add and whisk or shake until well blended:

¾ cup buttermilk
2 to 3 tablespoons fresh lime juice

1 tablespoon snipped fresh chives
1 tablespoon minced fresh cilantro or parsley
Salt and ground black pepper to taste

Taste and adjust the seasonings. Use immediately or cover and refrigerate.

Reduced-Fat Blue-Cheese Dressing

About 1½ cups

Puree in a small food processor or blender:

¾ cup buttermilk
¼ cup fat-free mayonnaise
¼ cup crumbled blue cheese

1 clove garlic, minced (optional)
Ground red pepper to taste

Transfer to a bowl and stir in:

1 tablespoon snipped fresh chives

Thin, if necessary, with additional:

Buttermilk or water

Taste and adjust the seasonings. Use immediately or cover and refrigerate.

Creamy Black-Olive Basil Dressing

About 1¾ cups

Puree in a food processor or blender:

¼ cup pitted Kalamata or other brine-cured black olives
¼ cup grainy mustard
1 teaspoon minced garlic

Add and pulse to combine:

¼ cup balsamic vinegar

Drizzle in with the machine running, and process until smooth:

¾ cup olive oil

Add and pulse to combine:

¼ cup coarsely chopped fresh basil
Salt and ground black pepper to taste

Use immediately or cover and refrigerate.

Creamy Chili Dressing

About 1½ cups

Chili dressing is a fine substitute for salsa. Try it with avocados, tomatoes, salad greens, cooked dried beans, chicken, or shrimp.

Whisk together in a small bowl or combine in a blender:

½ cup olive oil

¼ cup sour cream

Add and whisk together or blend to combine:

¼ cup fresh lime juice
¼ cup coarsely chopped fresh cilantro
2 tablespoons chili powder

2 teaspoons ground cumin
Salt and cracked black peppercorns to taste

Taste and adjust the seasonings. Use the dressing immediately or cover and refrigerate.

Clockwise from top: Creamy Chili Dressing, above; Creamy Black-Olive Basil Dressing, above; Creamy Blue-Cheese Dressing, 121

Roasted Red Pepper Dressing

About 1 ¾ cups

Roast, 79:

2 red bell peppers

Peel, seed, and coarsely chop. Puree in a food processor or blender. Add and pulse to blend:

¼ cup balsamic vinegar

¼ cup finely chopped fresh basil, thyme, or oregano, or a combination

2 teaspoons minced garlic

Salt and ground black pepper to taste

With the machine running, slowly pour through the feed tube and process until smooth:

¾ cup olive oil

Taste and adjust the seasonings. Use immediately or cover and refrigerate.

Feta Dressing (Reduced Fat)

About ½ cup

Feta is lower in fat than many other cheeses but still has plenty of flavor. Be sure to use the best-quality feta available.

Process in a blender or food processor until smooth:

2 ounces feta cheese, crumbled

¼ cup red wine vinegar

1 teaspoon minced fresh oregano

Salt and ground black pepper to taste

With the machine running, slowly pour through the feed tube and process until smooth:

2 tablespoons extra-virgin olive oil

Taste and adjust the seasonings. Use immediately or cover and refrigerate.

Tahini Dressing

About 2¼ cups

Tahini, the sesame-seed paste that is a staple of Middle Eastern cooking, is available in specialty food stores and some supermarkets. Because the sesame-seed paste separates (much like natural peanut butter), it is necessary to stir it thoroughly before using. This tahini dressing goes especially well with salads that include chickpeas. It also makes a great dip for raw vegetable crudités.

Whisk together in a small bowl:

1 cup tahini

½ cup water

Juice of 2 lemons, or to taste

3 cloves garlic, minced

1 tablespoon minced fresh cilantro, or to taste

1 teaspoon ground coriander

½ teaspoon ground cumin

Salt to taste

Ground red pepper to taste

Thin with water as necessary, especially when using as a dressing. Taste and adjust the seasonings. Use the dressing immediately or cover and refrigerate.

Goat Cheese Dressing (Reduced Fat)

About 1 cup

This dressing comes by its tang naturally—with the addition of goat cheese. The fresh white cheese substitutes for the more caloric, and more traditional, creamy dressing base of sour cream or mayonnaise.

Whisk together in a small bowl:

4 ounces soft fresh goat cheese, at room temperature
¼ cup buttermilk
2 teaspoons white wine vinegar
1 teaspoon Dijon mustard
1 teaspoon minced fresh thyme
1 teaspoon minced fresh parsley
Pinch of grated lemon zest
Salt and ground black pepper to taste

Thin, if necessary, with additional:

Buttermilk or water

Taste and adjust the seasonings. Use immediately or cover and refrigerate.

Yogurt Dill Dressing (Reduced Fat)

About ¾ cup

Vary this all-purpose creamy, reduced-fat dressing by using other fresh herbs, such as thyme, oregano, or mint, in place of the dill; substituting chives for the shallots; or adding a generous pinch of curry powder, ground cumin, or ground red pepper.

Whisk together in a small bowl:

½ cup nonfat yogurt
2 shallots, minced (opposite)
2 tablespoons finely snipped fresh dill
2 teaspoons Dijon mustard
Salt and ground black pepper to taste

Taste and adjust the seasonings. Use immediately or cover and refrigerate.

Guacamole Dressing

About 2 cups

This dressing goes well with any salad that includes seafood, particularly grilled salmon. You can also use it as a dip for tortilla chips, just like guacamole itself.

Whisk together in a medium bowl:

¼ cup fresh lime juice
¼ cup finely chopped fresh cilantro or parsley
2 teaspoons ground cumin
1 teaspoon minced garlic
1 teaspoon minced fresh chili peppers

Add in a slow, steady stream, whisking constantly, until smooth:

½ cup olive oil

Stir in:

2 avocados, peeled and finely diced
1 medium, ripe tomato, finely diced
Salt and cracked black peppercorns to taste

Taste and adjust the seasonings. Use immediately or cover and refrigerate.

Index

Bold type indicates that a recipe has an accompanying photograph.

ACKNOWLEDGMENTS

Special thanks to my wife and editor in residence, Susan; our indispensable assistant and comrade, Mary Gilbert; and our friends and agents, Gene Winick and Sam Pinkus. Much appreciation also goes to Simon & Schuster, Scribner, and Weldon Owen for their devotion to this project. Thank you Carolyn, Susan, Bill, Marah, John, Terry, Roger, Gaye, Val, Norman, and all the other capable and talented folks who gave a part of themselves to the Joy of Cooking All About series.

My eternal appreciation goes to the food experts, writers, and editors whose contributions and collaborations are at the heart of Joy—especially Stephen Schmidt. He was to the 1997 edition what Chef Pierre Adrian was to Mom's final editions of Joy. Thank you one and all.

Ethan Becker

FOOD EXPERTS, WRITERS, AND EDITORS
Selma Abrams, Jody Adams, Samia Ahad, Bruce Aidells, Katherine Alford, Deirdre Allen, Pam Anderson, Elizabeth Andoh, Phillip Andres, Alice Arndt, John Ash, Nancy Baggett, Rick and Deann Bayless, Lee E. Benning, Rose Levy Beranbaum, Brigit Legere Binns, Jack Bishop, Carole Bloom, Arthur Boehm, Ed Brown, JeanMarie Brownson, Larry Catanzaro, Val Cipollone, Polly Clingerman, Elaine Corn, Bruce Cost, Amy Cotler, Brian Crawley, Gail Damerow, Linda Dann, Deirdre Davis, Jane Spencer Davis, Erica De Mane, Susan Derecskey, Abigail Johnson Dodge, Jim Dodge, Aurora Esther, Michele Fagerroos, Eva Forson, Margaret Fox, Betty Fussell, Mary Gilbert, Darra Goldstein, Elaine Gonzalez, Dorie Greenspan, Maria Guarnaschelli, Helen Gustafson, Pat Haley, Gordon Hamersley, Melissa Hamilton, Jessica Harris, Hallie Harron, Nao Hauser, William Hay, Larry Hayden, Kate Hays, Marcella Hazan, Tim Healea, Janie Hibler, Lee Hofstetter, Paula Hogan, Rosemary Howe, Mike Hughes, Jennifer Humphries, Dana Jacobi, Stephen Johnson, Lynne Rossetto Kasper, Denis Kelly, Fran Kennedy, Johanne Killeen and George Germon, Shirley King, Maya Klein, Diane M. Kochilas, Phyllis Kohn, Aglaia Kremezi, Mildred Kroll, Loni Kuhn, Corby Kummer, Virginia Lawrence, Jill Leigh, Karen Levin, Lori Longbotham, Susan Hermann Loomis, Emily Luchetti, Stephanie Lyness, Karen MacNeil, Deborah Madison, Linda Marino, Kathleen McAndrews, Alice Medrich, Anne Mendelson, Lisa Montenegro, Cindy Mushet, Marion Nestle, Toby Oksman, Joyce O'Neill, Suzen O'Rourke, Russ Parsons, Holly Pearson, James Peterson, Marina Petrakos, Mary Placek, Maricel Presilla, Marion K. Pruitt, Adam Rapoport, Mardee Haidin Regan, Peter Reinhart, Sarah Anne Reynolds, Madge Rosenberg, Nicole Routhier, Jon Rowley, Nancy Ross Ryan, Chris Schlesinger, Stephen Schmidt, Lisa Schumacher, Marie Simmons, Nina Simonds, A. Cort Sinnes, Sue Spitler, Marah Stets, Molly Stevens, Christopher Stoye, Susan Stuck, Sylvia Thompson, Jean and Pierre Troisgros, Jill Van Cleave, Patricia Wells, Laurie Wenk, Caroline Wheaton, Jasper White, Jonathan White, Marilyn Wilkenson, Carla Williams, Virginia Willis, John Willoughby, Deborah Winson, Lisa Yockelson.

Weldon Owen wishes to thank the following people for their generous assistance and support in producing this book: Desne Border, Ina Chow, Ken DellaPenta, and Joan Olson.